EXPLANATION AND
UNDERSTANDING

CONTEMPORARY PHILOSOPHY

General Editor
Max Black, Cornell University

Induction and Hypothesis: A Study of the Logic of Confirmation.
By S. F. Barker.

Perceiving: A Philosophical Study.
By Roderick M. Chisholm.

The Moral Point of View: A Rational Basis of Ethics.
By Kurt Baier.

Religious Belief. By C. B. Martin.

Knowledge and Belief: An Introduction to the Logic of the Two Notions. By Jaakko Hintikka.

Reference and Generality: An Examination of Some Medieval and Modern Theories.
By Peter Thomas Geach.

Self-Knowledge and Self-Identity.
By Sydney Shoemaker.

God and Other Minds: A Study of the Rational Justification of Belief in God.
By Alvin Plantinga.

Explanation and Understanding.
By Georg Henrik von Wright.

EXPLANATION
AND
UNDERSTANDING

By *Georg Henrik von Wright*

Cornell University Press

ITHACA, NEW YORK

First published 1971

International Standard Book Number 0-8014-0644-7
Library of Congress Catalog Card Number 72-149576

PRINTED IN THE UNITED STATES OF AMERICA
BY VAIL-BALLOU PRESS, INC.

"... und tiefer als der Tag gedacht ..."
—NIETZSCHE, *Zarathustra*

To Norman Malcolm

Preface

This book has grown out of my interest in the theory of action, which in turn grew out of my interest in norms and values. To begin with, I was attracted by the formal-logical aspects of action concepts. This was a field in which little had previously been done, but the clearing of which seemed necessary if "deontic logic" was to stand on a firm footing. From the logic of action my interest shifted to the explanation of action. My thinking was deeply affected by Charles Taylor's book *The Explanation of Behaviour*. It made me realize how deep into the traditional problem-body, not only of philosophy of science but of philosophy generally, questions of explanation cut. So, eventually, what had been a study of action became a contribution to the old question of how the sciences of nature are related to the study of man.

The questions discussed here are controversial, much debated, and of great complexity. Never before have I felt so strongly the dangers of misunderstanding even on the terminological level. The nature of an author's opinion is far from clear from the wording of a few theses which he puts forward and defends. Thus, for example, I may be said to be anxious to defend a view according to which human actions *cannot* have causes. But many writers, both in past and present times, maintain that actions *can* be caused. Do I disagree with their views? Not necessarily. For those who think that actions have causes often use "cause" in a much broader sense than I do when I deny this. Or they may understand "action" differently. It may very well be, then, that "actions" in their sense have "causes" in my sense, or that "actions" in my sense have "causes" in theirs. I am not insisting that my use is either better or more natural as far as ordinary language goes.

At the same time it would be quite wrong to suggest that the difference between the views is merely terminological, if this means that a complete clarification of the terms must lead to complete agreement in substance. In the elucidations of meaning, new concepts, not less controversial than "cause" and "action," will be used. The one who affirms and the one who disputes that actions can have causes will probably assimilate, link, the two ideas differently with those other concepts. The one will emphasize distinctions that the other will tend to blur or overlook. The "causalist" will perhaps link intentions, motives, and reasons to causes, and actions to events. The "actionist" groups the concepts differently: motives and reasons with actions, and events with causes—and between the two groups he sees a sharp divide. The former may not wish to accord experimentation a crucial role in the formation of the *concept* of cause. Or at least he will not admit that, since experimentation is a mode of action, action is conceptually fundamental to causation. The "causalist" and the "actionist," in other words, knit differently the conceptual web against whose background they see the world—and they therefore see the world differently. When set in a historical perspective their world views become linked with the two traditions of thought which I try to describe and differentiate in Chapter I.

Preface

The first three chapters of this book were originally independent essays. They may still be said to be, relative to one another, self-contained. The fourth, however, is largely a sketch to show how patterns of explanation discussed abstractly in chapters II and III may be employed for explicative tasks in historiography and social science.

Preliminary versions of the second and third chapters were presented to various academic audiences from 1965 onwards. I am grateful for the challenge and stimulus which critical responses from my audiences have given to the further development of my ideas. The first synoptic presentation of the material contained in this book were my Tarner Lectures at Cambridge in autumn 1969. I wish to thank the Council of Trinity College, Cambridge, for inviting me to the lectureship. Without this external impetus, the results of my research in the area would not have matured into the form of a book. Extracts of a more finished version of the manuscript were presented in public lectures at Cornell in spring 1970. I am deeply indebted to the chairman of the Andrew D. White Professors-at-Large Program and general editor of the Contemporary Philosophy series, Professor Max Black, for the opportunities which were essential to the finishing and publication of my work.

GEORG HENRIK VON WRIGHT

Contents

xi

Contents

II. Causality and Causal Explanation

Contents

Contents

Contents

IV. Explanation in History and the Social Sciences

Contents

Contents

ation, as that of causal explanation, a matter of experience. The claim that history has an immanent goal transcends the boundaries of a "scientific" study of man and society.   165

EXPLANATION AND
UNDERSTANDING

I

Two Traditions

1. Scientific inquiry, seen in a very broad perspective, may be said to present two main aspects. One is the ascertaining and discovery of facts, the other the construction of hypotheses and theories. These two aspects of scientific activity are sometimes termed *descriptive* and *theoretical* science.

Theory-building can be said to serve two main purposes. One is to *predict* the occurrence of events or outcomes of experiments, and thus to anticipate new facts. The other is to *explain*, or to make intelligible facts which have already been recorded.

These classifications are useful for the purposes of a first approximation, but they must not be taken too rigidly. The discovery and description of facts cannot always be conceptually separated from a theory about them and is often an important step towards an understanding of their nature.[1] Prediction and explanation again are sometimes regarded as basically identical processes of scientific thinking—differing only in the time perspective, so to speak.[2] Prediction looks forward from what is

1

to what will come, explanation usually looks back from what is to what went before. But, it is argued, the terms of the predictive and the explicative relations are similar, and so is the relation linking them. The former are some facts, the latter is a law. This view of prediction and explanation, however, may be challenged.[3] To challenge it is to question the role of general laws in scientific explanation and to raise the problem of whether theory-building is intrinsically the same endeavor in the natural sciences and in the humanistic and social disciplines.

Some of the problems concerning the interrelation of the various concepts just mentioned—description, explanation, prediction, and theory—may usefully be considered in the light of intellectual history.

Two main traditions can be distinguished in the history of ideas, differing as to the conditions an explanation has to satisfy in order to be scientifically respectable. The one tradition is sometimes called *aristotelian*, the other *galilean*.[4] The names suggest that the first has very ancient roots in the intellectual history of man, while the second is of relatively recent origin. There is some truth in this, but it should be taken with a grain of salt. What I here call the galilean tradition has an ancestry going back beyond Aristotle to Plato.[5] One should also beware of thinking that the aristotelian tradition today represents merely the fading survival of obsolete elements from which science is gradually becoming "liberated."

As to their views of scientific explanation, the contrast between the two traditions is usually characterized as causal *versus* teleological explanation.[6] The first type of explanation is also called mechanistic,[7] the second finalistic. The galilean tradition in science runs parallel with the advance of the causal-mechanistic point of view in man's efforts to explain and predict phenomena, the aristotelian tradition with his efforts to make facts teleologically or finalistically understandable.

I shall not attempt to survey the development of the two traditions from their beginnings. Nor shall I try to assess their relative importance to the advancement of science. I shall restrict my *aperçu* in time to the era roughly from the mid-nineteenth century to the present day, with the emphasis on recent developments. I shall further restrict its scope to methodology, by which I mean the philosophy of scientific method.

2. The great awakening or revolution in the natural sciences during the late Renaissance and the Baroque era was to a certain extent paralleled in the nineteenth century in the systematic study of man, his history, languages, *mores*, and social institutions. The work of Ranke and Mommsen in historiography, Wilhelm von Humboldt, Rasmus Rask, Jacob Grimm in linguistics and philology, Tylor in social anthropology, is comparable to the achievements, two or three centuries earlier, of Copernicus and Kepler in astronomy, Galileo and Newton in physics, or Vesalius and Harvey in anatomy and physiology.

Since natural science was already established on the intellectual stage, and the humanistic studies with a scientific claim were newcomers, it was but natural that one of the chief issues of nineteenth-century methodology and philosophy of science concerned the relationship between these two main branches of empirical inquiry. The principal stands on this issue can be linked with the two main traditions in methodological thinking we have distinguished.

One stand is the philosophy of science most typically represented by Auguste Comte and John Stuart Mill. It is usually called *positivism*. The name was coined by Comte, but used

3

with due caution it is also appropriate for the position of Mill [8] and for an entire intellectual tradition extending from Comte and Mill not only down to the present day but also upward in the stream of time to Hume and the philosophy of the Enlightenment.

One of the tenets of positivism [9] is *methodological monism,* or the idea of the unity of scientific method amidst the diversity of subject matter of scientific investigation.[10] A second tenet is the view that the exact natural sciences, in particular mathematical physics, set a methodological ideal or standard which measures the degree of development and perfection of all the other sciences, including the humanities.[11] A third tenet, finally, is a characteristic view of scientific explanation.[12] Such explanation is, in a broad sense, "causal." [13] It consists, more specifically, in the subsumption of individual cases under hypothetically assumed general laws of nature,[14] including "human nature." [15] The attitude towards finalistic explanations, *i.e.* towards attempts to account for facts in terms of intentions, goals, purposes, is either to reject them as unscientific or to try to show that they can, when duly purified of "animist" or "vitalist" remains, be transformed into causal explanations.[16]

Through its emphasis on unity of method, on the mathematical ideal-type of a science, and on the importance of general laws to explanation, positivism is linked with that longer and more ramified tradition in the history of ideas which I have here called galilean.[17]

3. Another stand on the question of the relationship between the sciences of nature and of man was a reaction against positivism. The antipositivist philosophy of science which became prominent towards the end of the nineteenth century is a much more diversified and heterogenous trend than posi-

tivism. The name "idealism" which is sometimes used to characterize it is appropriate only for some facets of this trend. A better name for it seems to me to be *hermeneutics*. (See below, pp. 29ff.) Representatives of this type of thought included some eminent German philosophers, historians, and social scientists. Perhaps the best known of them are Droysen, Dilthey, Simmel, and Max Weber. Windelband and Rickert of the neo-kantian Baden School are related to them. The Italian Croce and the eminent British philosopher of history and art Collingwood may be said to belong to the idealist wing of this anti-positivist trend in methodology.

All these thinkers reject the methodological monism of positivism and refuse to view the pattern set by the exact natural sciences as the sole and supreme ideal for a rational understanding of reality. Many of them emphasize a contrast between those sciences which, like physics or chemistry or physiology, aim at generalizations about reproducible and predictable phenomena, and those which, like history, want to grasp the individual and unique features of their objects. Windelband coined the label "nomothetic" for sciences which search for laws, and "ideographic" for the descriptive study of individuality.[18]

The antipositivists also attacked the positivist view of explanation. The German historian-philosopher Droysen appears to have been the first to introduce a methodological dichotomy which has had great influence. He coined for it the names *explanation* and *understanding*, in German *Erklären* and *Verstehen*.[19] The aim of the natural sciences, he said, is to explain; the aim of history is to understand the phenomena which fall within its domain. These methodological ideas were then worked out to systematic fulness by Wilhelm Dilthey.[20] For the entire domain of the understanding method he used the name *Geisteswissenschaften.* There is no good equivalent in English, but it should be mentioned that the word was originally coined for the purpose of translating into German the English term "moral science." [21]

Ordinary usage does not make a sharp distinction between the words "explain" and "understand." Practically every explanation, be it causal or teleological or of some other kind, can be said to further our understanding of things. But "understanding" also has a psychological ring which "explanation" has not. This psychological feature was emphasized by several of the nineteenth-century antipositivist methodologists, perhaps most forcefully by Simmel who thought that understanding as a method characteristic of the humanities is a form of *empathy* (in German *Einfühlung*) or re-creation in the mind of the scholar of the mental atmosphere, the thoughts and feelings and motivations, of the objects of his study.[22]

It is not only through this psychological twist, however, that understanding may be differentiated from explanation. Understanding is also connected with *intentionality* in a way explanation is not. One understands the aims and purposes of an agent, the meaning of a sign or symbol, and the significance of a social institution or religious rite. This intentionalistic or, as one could perhaps also call it, semantic dimension of understanding has come to play a prominent role in more recent methodological discussion. (Cf. below, Sect. 10.) [23]

If one accepts a fundamental methodological cleavage between the natural sciences and the historical *Geisteswissenschaften,* the question will immediately arise of where the social and behavioral sciences stand. These sciences were born largely under the influence of a cross pressure of positivist and antipositivist tendencies in the last century. It is therefore not surprising that they should have become a battleground for the two opposed trends in the philosophy of scientific method. The application of mathematical methods to political economy and other forms of social study was an inheritance of the eighteenth-century Enlightenment which found favor with nineteenth-century positivists. Comte himself coined the name "sociology" for the scientific study of human society.[24] Of the two great sociologists of the turn of the century, Emile Durkheim was essentially a positivist as far as his methodology is concerned,[25] while in Max Weber a positivist coloring is combined with emphasis on teleology (*"zweckrationales Handeln"*) and empathic understanding (*"verstehende Soziologie"*).[26]

4. Hegel and Marx are two great philosophers of the past century who have had a profound and enduring influence, not least on ways of thinking about method, but whom it is difficult to place in relation to either nineteenth-century positivism or the reactions against positivism.[27] Hegelian and marxist thinking about method puts strong emphasis on laws, universal validity, and necessity.[28] In this it resembles, at least superficially, the positivist, (natural-)science-oriented trend. But the idea of law which figures in the writings of Hegel and Marx when they discuss, for example, the historical process, is very different from the idea of law which underlies ("galilean") causal explanations. Similarly, the dialectic schema of development through thesis, antithesis, and synthesis is not a *causal*(istic) pattern of thought.[29] The hegelian and marxist ideas of law and of development are closer to what we should call patterns of conceptual or logical connections.[30] In this respect they resemble the methodological ideas of an intentionalistic and teleological type expounded by such antipositivist philosophers as Croce and Collingwood, who were influenced by hegelianism.

Explanation and Understanding

Hegel thought of himself as a follower of Aristotle.[31] Unlike the Master Philosopher, Hegel had little understanding of natural science. In this the spirit of his thinking is alien to that of positivism and has close affinities with that of the philosophers of the *Geisteswissenschaften*. But notwithstanding this "humanist" as against "naturalist" emphasis, it seems to me true to say that Hegel is the great renewer—after the Middle Ages and therefore necessarily in opposition to the platonizing spirit of Renaissance and Baroque science—of an aristotelian tradition in the philosophy of method. For Hegel, as for Aristotle, the idea of law is primarily that of an intrinsic connection to be grasped through reflective understanding, not that of an inductive generalization established by observation and experiment. For both philosophers, explanation consists in making phenomena teleologically intelligible rather than predictable from knowledge of their efficient causes.[32] When it is seen in its affinity and relationship to Hegel, nineteenth-century antipositivist methodology as a whole can be linked with an older aristotelian tradition, superseded three centuries earlier by a new spirit in the philosophy of science whose most impressive champion was Galileo.[33]

5. The heyday of positivism in the middle of the nineteenth century was succeeded by an antipositivist reaction towards the end and round the turn of the century. But in the decades between the two world wars positivism returned, more vigorous than ever. The new movement was called neo-positivism or logical positivism, later also logical empiricism. The attribute "logical" was added to indicate the support which the revived positivism drew from the new developments in formal logic.

The revival of logic after half a millennium of decay and stagnation—from roughly 1350 to 1850 not counting the brilliant but isolated contributions of Leibniz in the seventeenth century—has in itself been of major importance to methodology and the philosophy of science. But formal logic can hardly be said to be intrinsically connected with positivism or with a positivist philosophy of science. The alliance between logic and positivism in this century is therefore a historical accident rather than a philosophical necessity.

The logical positivism of the 1920's and 1930's was a main, though by no means the sole, tributary out of which grew the broader current of philosophical thought nowadays commonly known as analytical philosophy. It would be quite wrong to label analytical philosophy as a whole a brand of positivism. But it is true to say that the contributions of analytical philosophy to methodology and philosophy of science have, until recently, been predominantly in the spirit of positivism, if by "positivism" one understands a philosophy advocating methodological monism, mathematical ideals of perfection, and a subsumption-theoretic view of scientific explanation. There are several reasons for this. One is connected with a bifurcation of analytic philosophy into two main substreams.

One is the trend called linguistic philosophy or ordinary language philosophy. Its main source of inspiration was the later philosophy of Wittgenstein and its flourishing center at Oxford in the 1950's. Of this subcurrent one might say that it is intrinsically disposed against positivism, though until recently this disposition remained latent rather than manifest. Ordinary language philosophy has, for understandable reasons, taken relatively little interest in the philosophy of science.

The other subcurrent is a completely different case. It is the heir to the logical atomism of Russell and the early Wittgenstein and to the neopositivism of the Vienna Circle. Its predominant interest can rightly be said to have been the philosophy of science. But, because of its very ancestry, its intrinsic disposition has been positivistic. It also largely shares with nineteenth-century positivism an implicit trust in progress through the advancement of science and the cultivation of a rationalist "social engineering" attitude to human affairs.[34]

Analytic philosophers of science were long concerned almost exclusively with questions of the foundations of mathematics and the methodology of the exact natural sciences. This must be understood partly against the background of the impact of (mathematical) logic on that type of philosophy. Gradually, however, the methodology of the behavioral and social sciences and of history has begun to interest analytic philosophers, no doubt partly as a consequence of the invasion of these sciences by exact methods. With this shift in the field of interest, analytic philosophy of science entered the traditional battle-ground between positivist and antipositivist methodology, and the old controversies flared up again in the mid-century. The immediate source for the revived debate was a modern version of the old positivist theory of scientific explanation.

6. The discussion of problems of explanation within the tradition of analytic philosophy received its decisive impetus from Carl Gustav Hempel's classic paper "The Function of General Laws in History," published in the *Journal of Philosophy* in 1942. Logical positivists and other analytical philosophers had already put forward views of explanation similar to those of Hempel.[35] Essentially, all these views are variants of the explanation theory espoused by the classics of positivism, in particular by Mill.

In retrospect, it seems almost an irony of fate that the fullest and most lucid formulation of the positivist theory of explanation should have been stated in connection with the subject matter for which, obviously, the theory is least suited, *viz.* history. But it is probably chiefly for that very reason that Hempel's paper has provoked such an immense amount of discussion and controversy.

The hempelian theory of explanation has become known as the Covering Law Model (or Theory). The name was invented by one of the theory's critics, William Dray.[36] An alternative, and perhaps better, name for it would be the Subsumption Theory of Explanation.

In a number of later publications Hempel has amplified, elucidated, and in some details modified his original opinions.[37] He has also distinguished between two submodels of the general covering law model of explanation. We shall here call them the Deductive-Nomological and the Inductive-Probabilistic models.[38] The first can be schematically described as follows:

Let E be an event which is known to have taken place on some occasion and which stands in need of explanation. Why did E happen? In order to answer the question, we point to certain other events or states of affairs $E_1, \ldots, E_m$ and to one or several general propositions or laws $L_1, \ldots, L_n$ such that the occurrence of E (on the occasion in question) follows logically from those laws and the fact that those other events (states) have occurred (obtain).

E in the above schematic description of Hempel's deductive-nomological model is called the *explanandum* or *explicandum*. I shall also call it the *object* of explanation. $E_1, \ldots, E_m$ I shall call the *explanans* or *explicatum*. They can also be called the *basis* of the explanation. $L_1, \ldots, L_n$ are the "covering laws" under which the explanation subsumes the *explanans* and the *explanandum*.[39]

One might ask whether Hempel's model applies only to

objects of explanation which are events. Often we are anxious to know, not why an event has taken place, but why a certain state of affairs obtains or fails to obtain. This case, too, can obviously be fitted into Hempel's mold. It may even be regarded as the more fundamental case in that the notion of an event can be analyzed (defined) with the aid of the notion of a state of affairs. An event, one could say, is a pair of successive states.[40]

Another question which our description of the model raises is whether the events or states $E_1, \ldots , E_m$, which constitute the basis of the explanation, must have occurred or come into being earlier than E, or whether they can be simultaneous with or perhaps even later than E. This is an important question, some aspects of which we shall discuss later. When the events E_i are earlier than the object of explanation E, we shall refer to them as *antecedents* of E.

Hempel's own, now famous, example of a deductive-nomological explanation is typically one in which the *explanandum* is an event and the *explanans* consists of antecedent events and states.[41] Why did the radiator of my car burst during the night? The tank was brim-full of water; the lid was tightly screwed on; no antifreeze liquid had been added; the car had been left in the courtyard; the temperature during the night fell unexpectedly to well below zero. These were the antecedents. In combination with the laws of physics—in particular the law that the volume of water expands when it freezes—they explain the bursting of the radiator. From knowledge of the antecedents and the laws we could have *predicted* the event with certainty. This is indeed a good example of an explanation, but *not* of the types of explanation for which historians look.

12

Two Traditions

Our discussion of the subsumption theory of explanation will be limited almost exclusively to the deductive-nomological model. A brief presentation, however, will be given here of the inductive-probabilistic model, on which we shall also make a critical comment.[42]

The object of an inductive-probabilistic explanation, too, is an individual event E. The basis is a set of other events or states E_1, . . . , E_m. The covering law, the "bridge" or "tie" connecting the basis with the object of explanation, is a probability-hypothesis to the effect that on an occasion when E_1, . . . , E_m are instantiated, it is *highly probable* that E will occur.

Here it is pertinent to ask in what sense, if any, could this type of basis and covering law be said to *explain* the actual occurrence of an event? [43]

What makes a deductive-nomological explanation "explain," is, one might say, that it tells us why E *had to* be (occur), why E was *necessary* once the basis is there and the laws are accepted. But it is part and parcel of an inductive-probabilistic explanation that it admits the possibility that E might have *failed* to occur. It therefore leaves room for an additional quest for explanation: why did E, on this occasion, actually occur and why did it not fail to occur? It would be the task of a deductive-nomological explanation to answer *this* question. Sometimes we can answer it. This happens when we are able to add to the basis of explanation some further event or state E_{m+1} such that, according to accepted laws, an event of the kind E will occur on all occasions when events of the kind E_1, . . . , E_{m+1} jointly materialize.[44] One could now make a distinction and say that, failing such additional information which gives us a deductive-nomological explanation of E, we have not explained why E *occurred*, but only why E *was to be expected*.

Let there be a probability law (hypothesis) to the effect that, when E_1, . . . , E_m are instantiated, it is probable to degree p that E will occur, where p is a mediocre or low probability. Then no one would say that the probability law explains the actual occurrence of E. But one might be able to use the information contained in the law for deriving another probability law which says that it is *highly probable* that the *relative frequency* with which E will occur on so many occasions when $E_1, \ldots, E_m$ are instantiated is near the value p. The occurrence of E with this relative frequency is another individual event. This event is here to be expected.

There is a characteristic use of probability laws for predicting with high probability relative frequencies of occurrences of events, whose probabilities are any value—high, low, or mediocre. The case when the frequency-event is the occurrence of E itself, *i.e.* the occurrence of E with a relative frequency 1 on a given occasion, is a limiting case of a more general pattern for using probabilities in making predictions. The hempelian inductive-probabilistic model, I should therefore say, is just a special instance of a characteristic use of the probability-calculus for predictive purposes.

The two models are much more different than is often thought. It is a primary function of the deductive-nomological model to explain why certain things happened. Therefore it also tells us, secondarily, why these things were to be expected. They could have been expected, *since* they had to happen. With the inductive-probabilistic model the roles are reversed. It explains in the first place why things which happened were to be expected (or not to be expected). Only in a secondary sense does it explain why things happened, *viz.* "because" they were highly probable. It seems to me better, however, not to say that the inductive-probabilistic model explains what happens, but to say only that it justifies certain expectations and predictions.

This is not to deny the existence of (genuine) explanation patterns in which probability plays a characteristic role. One such pattern is the following:

Let there be a hypothesis to the effect that the probability of the event E on a random instantiation of the data $E_1, \ldots, E_m$ is such and such, say p. The event is found to occur with a relative frequency markedly different from p in a (large) set of instantiations of the data. Why this difference? There are two principal ways of accounting for it. One is to attribute it to "chance." This way is always open to us, but on the whole is only a last resort. The other way is to look for and discover a further datum E_{m+1} which was also instantiated in the set of instantiations of $E_1, \ldots, E_m$. A probability p', different from p, is associated with the occurrence of E on an instantiation of $E_1, \ldots, E_m, E_{m+1}$. This probability, let us assume, is such that the relative frequency with which E actually occurred in the set of instantiations was (in the sense explained before) to be expected. This is like finding a *cause* (E_{m+1}) of the observed discrepancy between frequency and probability (p). The procedure for testing the correctness of the suggested explanation is similar to the procedure which we shall later describe under the name of *causal analysis*. One could call it *probabilistic* causal analysis. It occupies an important place in the methodology of explanation, but will not be discussed in further detail in this book.[45]

7. Hempel's (deductive-nomological) explanation model does not mention the notions of cause and effect. The model covers a broader range, of which causal explanations are meant to form a subrange.[46] It is debatable whether all causal explanations really conform to Hempel's schema. It may also be asked whether the schema really carries the weight of an explanation unless the covering laws are causal.

The answer to both questions depends upon the view one takes of the nature of causation. I shall try to show that there are important uses of "cause" in connection with explanation which do not fit the covering law model. But there are also important uses which fit it. It seems to me, moreover, clarifying to reserve the term "causal explanation" for such uses. It is then indisputably true that causal explanation conforms to the covering law model, though not necessarily to that simplified version of it which we presented in the preceding section.

The primary test of the claim to universal validity for the subsumption theory of explanation is whether the covering law model also captures teleological explanations.

One could divide the domain traditionally claimed for teleology into two subprovinces. One is the domain of the notions of *function, purpose*(fullness) and *"organic wholes"* ("systems"). The other is that of *aiming* and *intentionality*.[47] Function and purpose figure prominently in the biological sciences, intentionality in the behavioral sciences, social study, and historiography. But the domains of biology and of behavioral science largely overlap and so, of course, do the domains of function, purpose, and wholes on the one hand and that of aiming and intentionality on the other. To distinguish them may nevertheless be useful.

In 1943, a year after the publication of Hempel's paper, an important article by Rosenblueth, Wiener, and Bigelow appeared entitled "Behavior, Purpose, and Teleology." [48] This is another milestone in the modern history of explanation theory. The authors wrote independently of Hempel. But their contribution, seen in the historical perspective, should be regarded as an effort to extend the "causalist" [49] and with it the subsumption-theoretic view of explanation to biology and behavioral science.

A key notion in the "causalist" account of purposefulness, proposed by the three authors of the article,[50] is *negative feedback*. A system within which a cause-factor, say a heater, produces an effect, say the rise of temperature of a room, may be associated with another system such that a "failure" in the effect of the first system, say a drop in the temperature below a certain point, produces a "correction," say increased heating activity, in the operation of its cause-factor. The effect-factor of the second system then gives the operation of the cause-factor of the first system an "appearance of teleology." Yet both systems operate according to causal laws. The effects within both are explained on the basis of "initial conditions" constituted by the cause-factors with the aid of covering laws, linking the causes with their effects.

The authors of the article advanced the thesis that purposefulness can be explained in general by means of some such concatenation of causal systems.[51] The system with the correlated feedback mechanism is called homeostatic or self-regulating. Such mechanisms are highly characteristic of living organisms. For example, the temperature control in vertebrates is a case of a "heater" with a "thermostat."

The analysis of teleology proposed by Rosenblueth, Wiener, and Bigelow appears to agree with a subsumption-theoretic view of scientific explanation. It is not clear, however, whether the explanation pattern of this analysis is precisely that of the hempelian deductive-nomological schema as explained earlier. In order to see whether this is so, the analysis must be further elaborated. Important contributions to the logical analysis of self-regulating and other teleological processes have subsequently been made by several authors. Prominent among them are Braithwaite and Nagel.[52]

The general study of system control and of steering mechanisms, of which homeostasis is only an example, is known as *cybernetics*. It has had a great, not to say revolutionizing, influence on modern science, particularly on biology and engineering. Some think it constitutes a scientific contribution of the mid-century comparable in impact to the revolution in physics brought about by relativity and quantum theories in the early decades of the century.[53] As I see it, the significance

17

of this contribution to methodology has been a big advance, in the spirit of the galilean tradition, for the "causalist" and "mechanist" point of view. At the same time it has reinforced some of the main tenets of the positivist philosophy of science, in particular the unitary view of method and the subsumption theory of explanation. In quarters hostile to positivism this is sometimes denied by pointing to the vast differences between cybernetic systems and mechanistic systems of a more traditional and simpler type. Such differences undoubtedly exist.[54] They are reflected in the difference between the schema which explains the working of the cybernetic steering and control mechanisms and the more "simple-minded" schematism of the hempelian covering law model. But the differences here, I should say, are essentially in degree of complexity and logical sophistication of the models, not in the basic principles of explanation or in the view of the nature of scientific laws.

8. The notion of a law of nature, and of lawlike uniformities generally, holds a prominent place in the positivist philosophy of science.[55] Hempel's explanation models are typically "positivist" in this respect.

A more or less clearly articulated view of the *nature* of natural and other scientific laws has also been characteristic of positivism. According to this view, roughly speaking, laws enunciate the regular or uniform concomitance (correlation) of phenomena, *i.e.* features appearing in objects, states which obtain, or events which happen. The prototype instance of a law is either a universal implication ("all A are B") or a probabilistic correlation. Ideally, the phenomena connected by law should be logically independent. This requirement is roughly equivalent with the idea that the truth-value of laws is not a matter of logical necessity, but contingent upon the testimony of experience.[56] And since any law's claim to truth always transcends the experience which has actually been recorded, laws are in principle never completely verifiable.

Consider the following search for an explanation: Why is this bird black? Answer: It is a raven and all ravens are black. The answer accords with Hempel's deductive-nomological schema. But does it really explain why the bird is black? [57] Unless we are, as philosophers, wedded to the view that any subsumption of an individual case under a general proposition is an explanation, I think we instinctively doubt whether the answer is positive. We should like to know why ravens are black, what it is about them that "is responsible for" the color which, so we are told, is characteristic of them all. What is required, if our search for an explanation is to be satisfied, is that the basis of the explanation be somehow more strongly related to the object of explanation than simply by the law stating the universal concomitance of the two characteristics ravenhood and blackness.

There are two ways, it seems, in which this requirement could be satisfied. One is to look for a "cause" of the blackness of ravens, *i.e.* for some other characteristic of birds of this species which accounts for their color. The other is to give the suggested answer explicative force by declaring that blackness is, in fact, a defining characteristic of the species raven. To accept either answer is to regard the concomitance of the two features as not merely *universal,* but also, in some way, *necessary.*

The second approach confronts us with a view of natural laws which may be regarded as an alternative to the classic positivist view. According to this alternative conception, a scientific law can be immune to refutation by experience since its truth is analytical, logical. Agreement with the law is then a standard whereby individual cases are classified as falling, or not falling, under the generic phenomena connected by the law. All *A* are *B*, so if a thing purporting to be an *A* is found not to be *B*, then it is not really an *A* after all. Such standards for judging things are man-made agreements adopted in the process of concept formation. This view is therefore called *conventionalism*.[58]

When carried to their extremes, positivism and conventionalism are opposed views, in roughly the same sense in which extreme empiricism and extreme rationalism are opposed. But it is relatively easy to find a compromise between the extremes. A sensible positivist will agree that some scientific principles have the character of analytic truths while others are clearly empirical generalizations. He will note, moreover, that the border between the two categories has often fluctuated in the course of the historical development of a science.[59]

The conventionalist view of scientific laws, one might say, contains no conceptual elements which are alien to a positivist philosophy of science. Although conventionalism often attacked positivism, and vice versa, it was also felt that the two positions have much in common.[60] A common tenet of both views of scientific laws is that they deny the existence of a "middle" thing, sometimes called *natural necessity*, distinct from empirical generality on the one hand and logical necessity on the other.

For the same reason both positivism and conventionalism would deny that causal laws acquire their "explicative force" from the alleged fact that they state necessary connections between events in nature. To question the idea that universal truth must be either accidental (contingent, empirical) *or logically* necessary is a much more serious challenge to positivism than that presented by conventionalism.

This challenge, however, is traditional and is associated

with the opposition between the "aristotelian" and "galilean" trends in the philosophy of science. It is of particular interest here to note that it has emerged, acquiring a new urgency, within analytical philosophy itself, where it springs from two sources.

One is the rebirth, in the mid-century, of interest in *modal logic* and in the philosophy of the modal concepts. Philosophical logicians have become familiar with the view that the *logically* necessary and possible is only a *species* of a more comprehensive *genus* within which a variety of forms of necessity and possibility may be distinguished. The revival of modal logic has not in itself rehabilitated the notion of natural necessity as distinct from logical necessity and "mere" accidental generality. The idea remains controversial and is regarded by many analytical philosophers as suspect or definitely unsound. But modal logic has paved the way for a change in the positivist view of natural laws that was long accepted by analytical philosophers.[61]

A more immediate challenge to the accepted view of natural laws in the positivist tradition has come from the problem of *counterfactual conditionals*. This problem was posed by the classic papers of Chisholm (1946) and Goodman (1947). Since then it has been discussed in innumerable articles and books. Simplifying somewhat, its relevance to the problem of the nature of laws is as follows:

Sometimes our conviction, if we have one, that if it had not been the case that *p* then it would have been the case that *q*, is grounded on our belief in a nomic[62] or lawlike connection between the (generic) propositions *p* and *q*. Not just any valid universal implication connecting the two propositions would suffice as a ground. The question then arises of how to characterize lawlikeness or how to distinguish (nonlogical) nomic connection from "accidental" universal concomitance.[63] In an essay some fifteen years ago I argued that the notion of a counterfactual conditional is itself involved in this distinction —and therefore cannot be elucidated by means of it.[64] The "moral" to be drawn from the discussion of the problem of counterfactual conditionals is that the hallmark of nomic connection, lawlikeness, is *necessity and not universality*.[65] If this is correct, it shatters the positivist conception of law, though not necessarily the validity of the subsumption theory of explanation. I shall not discuss counterfactual conditionals here, but I hope to be able to throw a little more light on the nature of the "necessity" which makes some universal regularities nomic.

9. How deep into the province of teleology do cybernetic explanations penetrate? Do they extend beyond the frontiers of biology into the sciences of man? One could answer this last question by pointing to the great impact of cybernetic thinking on economics, social psychology, and even on the theory of law.[66] But this answer is not very illuminating. It does not tell us whether the use in these fields of ideas borrowed from cybernetics gives us explanations of the subsumption-theoretic type. My own surmise is that on the whole they do not. If I am right in this and also in thinking that the cybernetic explanations of homeostatic systems *etc.* in biological science do conform to subsumption-theoretic patterns, then the "cybernetics" of social science differs much more from that of biology than the assimilation of various research activities under this common heading might suggest.

The aspects of teleology captured by cybernetic explanations conforming to a covering law model are, I think, primarily the aspects void of intentionality. Among things to which intentionality is attributed *actions* occupy a prominent place. The final test of universal validity of the subsumption theory of explanation is whether it can successfully account for the explanation of actions.

Many analytic philosophers, perhaps the majority, think the theory passes the test. Actions are prompted by motives; the force of motives lies in the fact that agents are disposed to follow characteristic patterns of behavior; such patterns (dispositions) provide the "laws" linking the motives to the action in the individual case. This is a consciously oversimplified account of an idea which in more or less sophisticated variations continues to exercise a strong fascination over the philosophic imagination.[67] It is related to the idea that actions have causes, and thus also related to a determinist position in the old question of "the freedom of the will."

There is, however, also opposition among analytic philosophers to this idea of the validity of a subsumption-theoretic model of explanation of action.

One line of opposition has come from (analytic) philosophers engaged in the methodology of history. Here the critique has focused on the role of general laws in history—the theme which provided the very title of Hempel's paper, in which the covering law model was first clearly articulated.

Why is it that the explanations which historians actually give seldom, if ever, make reference to general laws? Supporters of the subsumption theory of historical explanation have, of course, been well aware of this. Their reactions to it, however, have varied a great deal.

In Hempel's view the reason why the full formulation of general laws is missing from historical explanations is primarily that the laws are too complex and our knowledge of them not sufficiently precise. Explanations given by historians are in a characteristic sense elliptical or incomplete. They are, strictly speaking, only *explanation sketches*. "An explanatory account," Hempel says, "may suggest, perhaps quite vividly and persuasively, the general outline of what, it is hoped, can eventually be supplemented so as to yield a more closely reasoned argument based on explanatory hypotheses which are indicated more fully." [68]

According to Popper, another prominent representative of the subsumption theory of explanation, the reason why general laws are not formulated in historical explanations is that the laws are too trivial to deserve explicit mention. We know them and take them for granted implicitly.[69]

A radically different view of the role of laws in historical explanations is expounded by William Dray in his important book *Laws and Explanation in History*, published in 1957. The reason why historical explanations do not normally make reference to laws is not that the laws are so complex and obscure that we must be content with a mere sketch, nor that they are too trivial to deserve mention. The reason, according to Dray, is simply that historical explanations do not rely on general laws at all.

Consider, *e.g.*, the statement that Louis XIV died unpopular, because he pursued policies detrimental to French national interests.[70] How could a covering law theorist defend his claim that there is a law implicit in the explanation? A general law which tells us that *all* rulers who . . . become unpopular, would provide a covering model of the case under discussion only if so many limiting and qualifying conditions were added to it that, in the end, it would be equivalent to saying that all rulers who pursue exactly similar policies to those of Louis XIV under exactly similar conditions to those which prevailed in France and the other countries affected by Louis's policies, become unpopular. If the exact similarity of policies and prevailing conditions is not specified in generic terms, this statement is no "law" at all, since of necessity it has only one instance, *viz.* that of Louis XIV. If the conditions of similarity are specified—which would hardly be possible in practice—we should have a genuine law, but the only instance of this law would be the one it is supposed to "explain." To maintain the law would therefore in either case amount only to a reaffirmation of what has already been stated, *viz.* that the cause of the aging Louis's unpopularity were his unlucky foreign policies.

Dray's criticism of the role of general laws in historical explanations thus leads to a complete rejection of the covering law model. It is illuminating to compare Dray's *Laws and Explanation in History* with Gardiner's *The Nature of Historical Explanation*, which was published five years earlier (1952). As I understand the two authors, their "methodological intentions" are to a large extent similar. But whereas Gardiner's intentions are badly thwarted by the dominant, though perhaps implicit, influence of a positivist philosophy of science, Dray succeeds admirably in breaking the fetters of positivism in contemporary "analytic" philosophy of history. He achieves this "negatively" through his critique of the covering law model as a tool for historical explanation, and "positively" through his insistence on the *sui generis* character of explanation models for human action. The critique is by far the strongest aspect of Dray's work. The positive contributions reflect the groping nature of an "analytic" philosophy of action, then still in its first beginnings.

To explain an action is, in Dray's view, to show that the action was the appropriate or rational thing to do on the occasion under consideration.[71] Dray calls this *rational explana-*

tion. He does not succeed in making its nature very clear. He thinks, quite rightly it seems to me, that this type of explanation has logical peculiarities of its own. But he obscures his own point unnecessarily by trying to find these peculiarities in an element of valuation rather than in a type of teleology.[72]

Dray's explanation model resembles traditional ideas about the methodological role of empathy and understanding. His book does not make contact with more recent continental philosophy of the *Geisteswissenschaften*. Instead there is an interesting link with the hegelian trend in Collingwood (and Oakeshott).[73]

Elizabeth Anscombe's *Intention* appeared the same year as Dray's book. It made the notion of intentionality central to subsequent discussion of the philosophy of action among analytic philosophers.[74]

Though not directly concerned with the theory of explanation, Miss Anscombe's book has made two important contributions to this field too. The first is her observation that behavior which is intentional under one description of it, need not be intentional under another. It thus makes a difference to the explanation of a given item of behavior how it is described, *i.e.* understood as being an action. This is a case when the distinction between explanation and understanding becomes conceptually significant. (Cf. below, Ch. III, Sect. 2, and Ch. IV, Sect. 1.)

Miss Anscombe has also drawn attention to the peculiar logical character of the reasoning called in traditional terminology *practical syllogisms*. The idea goes back to Aristotle and was, Miss Anscombe says, one of his best discoveries, though one which later philosophy has lost through misinterpretation.[75] The clue to a correct interpretation, however, is not easy to find. Aristotle's own treatment of the topic is very unsystematic and his examples are often confusing. *One* way of reconstructing the main idea here is the following: The starting point or major premise of the syllogism mentions some wanted thing or end of action; the minor premise relates some action to this thing, *roughly* as a means to the end; the conclusion, finally, consists in use of this means to secure that end. Thus, as in a theoretical inference the affirmation of the premises leads of necessity to the affirmation of the conclusion, in a practical inference assent to the premises entails action in accordance with them.[76]

I think Miss Anscombe is right in saying that the practical syllogism is not a form of demonstration and that it is a reasoning different *in kind* from the proof syllogism.[77] But its peculiarities and relation to theoretical reasoning are complex and remain obscure.

Practical reasoning is of great importance to the explanation and understanding of action. It is a tenet of the present work that the practical syllogism provides the sciences of man with something long missing from their methodology: an explanation model in its own right which is a definite alternative to the subsumption-theoretic covering law model.[78] Broadly speaking, what the subsumption-theoretic model is to causal explanation and explanation in the natural sciences, the practical syllogism is to teleological explanation and explanation in history and the social sciences.

The works of Anscombe and Dray reflect the increasing interest within analytic philosophy in the concept of action and in forms of practical discourse. These pioneer works have been followed by a number of further contributions.[79] But it was not until the appearance of Charles Taylor's important book *The Explanation of Behaviour* in 1964 that this new line in analytic philosophy became linked with explanation theory

27

in psychology and the other behavioral sciences. Like the contributions of cybernetics, but in a very different spirit, Taylor's work has revived the debate concerning teleology in the philosophy of science. One can characterize their difference in spirit as one between a galilean and an aristotelian view of purposive behavior.

The efforts and ideas of analytic philosophers of action have not failed to provoke reaction on the part of philosophers of a more positivist turn of mind. The applicability of causal categories to the explanation of action and behavior generally has been forcefully defended also by a number of recent authors.[80]

A position somewhat similar to Dray's in the "analytic" philosophy of history is held by Peter Winch in the "analytic" philosophy of the social sciences. His work *The Idea of a Social Science,* published in 1958, is, like Dray's book, an attack on positivism and a defense of an understanding of social phenomena by methods different in principle from those of the natural sciences. The tradition background of Winch's work is partly the "understanding" methodology of Max Weber and partly the hegelian trend represented in England by Collingwood and Oakeshott. The major influence, however, comes from the later Wittgenstein.

Winch's book can be said to center on the question of the criteria of social behavior (action). The social scientist must understand the "meaning" of the behavioral data which he registers in order to turn them into social facts. He achieves this understanding by describing (interpreting) the data in terms of the concepts and rules which determine the "social reality" of the agents whom he studies. The description, and explanation, of social behavior must employ the same conceptual framework as the social agents themselves. For this reason the social scientist cannot remain an outsider in relation to his object of study in the same sense in which a natural scientist can. *This* is the core of conceptual truth, one could say, in the psychologistic doctrine of "empathy." Empathic understanding is not a "feeling"; it is an ability to participate in a "form of life." [81]

Winch can be said to investigate the *a priori* of the method(s) of social science. In this sense his book is a contribution to methodology.[82] Some of Winch's critics seem to think that he regards sociology as an *a priori* science, *i.e.* as a study which explains and understands social phenomena by *a priori* methods. This is a gross misunderstanding.[83]

Winch's book is difficult and obscure. It is also one-sided, it seems to me, in that it puts too much emphasis on the importance of rules to the understanding of societal behavior. One misses in it the aspect of intentionality and teleology.[84]

10. A challenge to positivist methodology and philosophy of science has thus arisen within the mainstream of analytical philosophy, particularly after the appearance of the three works by Anscombe, Dray, and Winch. The years of their publication, 1957–1958, may be said to mark a turning of the tide. The critics of positivism among analytic philosophers have usually been writers whose thinking was inspired by the philosophy of the later Wittgenstein. An orientation to phenomenology and other brands of nonanalytic philosophy on the European continent can also be seen in some of them.[85]

This reorientation is to some extent paralleled in continental philosophy by developments disclosing affinities with analytical philosophy. I am thinking chiefly on the coming to prominence in the 1960's of the current which calls itself hermeneutic or hermeneutic-dialectic philosophy.[86]

There are two features of hermeneutics which are specially

noteworthy as regards affinities with analytical philosophy. The first is the central place held in it by the idea of *language* and by language-oriented notions such as meaning, intentionality, interpretation, and understanding.[87] This is reflected in the very name "hermeneutics," which means the art of interpretation.[88] The problems which occupy hermeneutic philosophers are largely the problems which also pervade the philosophy of Wittgenstein, particularly in its later phases.[89] It would not be surprising if this affinity, once it becomes clearly recognized, should lead to an impact of Wittgenstein on philosophy on the European continent comparable in degree, if not in kind, to his influence on the Vienna school of logical positivism in the 1930's and on the Oxford school of linguistic analysis in the 1950's.

The second feature of hermeneutic philosophy which makes it more congenial to philosophers of the analytic tradition than some other offshoots of the phenomenological stem is its concern with methodology and philosophy of science.[90] In explicit opposition to positivism's idea of the unity of science, hermeneutic philosophy defends the *sui generis* character of the interpretative and understanding methods of the *Geisteswissenschaften*. In this it revives and continues the intellectual inheritance of neokantian and neohegelian antipositivism from the decades around the turn of the century.

"Understanding," in terms of hermeneutic philosophy, should be distinguished from empathy or *Einfühlung*. It is a semantic rather than a psychological category. (Cf. above, p. 6.) The charge so often made by positivist philosophers that understanding is only a heuristic device, which may be useful for finding an explanation but which is not constitutive of the conceptual nature of the explanation model itself, may be valid against some earlier and outmoded versions of the methodology of empathy.[91] But it is not a fair objection against the methodology of understanding as such.

As noted above (Sect. 4) it is difficult to determine the position of Hegel and Marx in relation to positivist and antipositivist nineteenth-century philosophy of science. Something similar holds true of marxism as a mainstream of modern thought. After the Russian Revolution marxist philosophy was much absorbed in inner struggles for orthodoxy and gradually assumed a monolithic and stiffened appearance. But it is obviously rising again to intellectual prominence. It seems, moreover, that one can discern two main trends in this quarter.[92]

One is predominantly a philosophy of science fostered in the spirit of dialectical materialism. It has recently received fresh impetus from cybernetics and systems-theory and from the applications generally of mathematical tools to the life and behavioral sciences.[93] It is not surprising that "the causalization of teleology" should have a strong appeal to marxist materialists.[94] Differences in tradition notwithstanding, this trend in marxism has affinities with the branch of philosophy of science in the West which is the spiritual heir to logical positivism and the unity of science movement.[95] It is sometimes called "positivist," but more often "scientistic" marxism.[96]

The second trend within contemporary marxism is the philosophical anthropology which also calls itself socialist humanism.[97] Its sources of inspiration are partly in the writings of the young Marx, but even more perhaps in the philosophy of Hegel.[98] Its dialectic seems closer to that of hermeneutic philosophy than to the "materialism" of orthodox marxism.[99] Its anthropology and humanist political and social philosophy has affinities with existentialism, particularly with the later philosophy of Sartre, which in turn is oriented towards Marx and

Hegel.[100] Its philosophy of science is sometimes a defense of the sciences of man against the monistic pretensions of a thinking moulded under the impact of the progress of natural science and technology.

I have tried to relate some developments in the philosophy of scientific method to two great traditions in the history of ideas. We have seen how in the last hundred years philosophy of science has successively clung to one or the other of two basically opposed positions. After Hegel came positivism; after the antipositivist and partly neohegelian reaction around the turn of the century came neopositivism; now the pendulum is again swinging towards the aristotelian thematics which Hegel revived.

It would surely be an illusion to think that truth itself unequivocally sided with one of the two opposed positions. In saying this I am not thinking of the triviality that both positions contain some truth and that a compromise can be achieved on some questions. This may be so. But there is also a basic opposition, removed from the possibility both of reconciliation and of refutation—even, in a sense, removed from truth. It is built into the choice of primitives, of basic concepts for the whole argumentation. This choice, one could say, is "existential." It is a choice of a point of view which cannot be further grounded.

There is nevertheless dialogue between the positions, and a kind of progress. The temporary dominance of one of the two trends is usually the result of a breakthrough following a period of criticism of the other trend. What emerges after the breakthrough is never merely a restoration of something which was there before, but also bears the impress of the ideas through whose criticism it has emerged. The process illustrates what

Hegel described with the words *aufgehoben* and *aufbewart,* perhaps best rendered in English as "superseded" and "retained." The position which is in process of becoming superseded usually wastes its polemical energies on fighting already outmoded features in the opposed view, and tends to see what is retained in the emerging position as only a deformed shadow of its own self. This is what happens, for example, when positivist philosophers of science in our days object to *Verstehen* with arguments perhaps valid against Dilthey or Collingwood, or when they mistake Wittgenstein's philosophy of psychology for just another form of behaviorism.

II

Causality and
Causal Explanation

1. Philosophers have long been accustomed to making a distinction between the relation of cause and effect on the one hand and the relation of ground and consequence on the other. The first is factual and empirical, the second conceptual and logical. Before the distinction became current, it was often ignored or blurred—particularly by the rationalist thinkers of the seventeenth century. When it became more clearly articulated, thanks not least to Hume,[1] new problems arose. Perhaps all causal relations are factual. But, quite certainly, not all factual relations are causal. What, then, are the other distinguishing features of causal relations—in addition to their being empirical? According to Hume the relation between cause and effect is a regular sequence in time of (instantiations of) generic phenomena. That the regularity will continue to hold in the future is an inductive generalization, based on past experience.[2]

34

Causality and Causal Explanation

Since Hume, causation has been something of a problem child of epistemology and the philosophy of science. Many efforts have been made to show either that Hume's view of causation was mistaken or that, if one accepts his view, the problem of induction which it leaves open—also often called "the Problem of Hume"—can be satisfactorily solved.[3] These efforts have, on the whole, been unsuccessful, and the unsatisfactory state of the problem of induction has been called "the scandal of Philosophy." [4]

These troubles are probably *one* of the reasons why some philosophers have insisted that the idea of causation plays only an insignificant role in science and may eventually be exorcised from scientific thinking altogether.[5] The philosophical difficulties about causation need not then be a burden on the philosophy of science. This opinion was expressed forcefully by Bertrand Russell in his famous essay "On the Notion of Cause." With his characteristic wit Russell wrote: "All philosophers, of every school, imagine that causation is one of the fundamental axioms or postulates of science, yet, oddly enough, in advanced sciences such as gravitational astronomy, the word 'cause' never occurs. . . . The law of causality, I believe, like much that passes muster among philosophers, is a relic of a bygone age, surviving, like the monarchy, only because it is erroneously supposed to do no harm." [6] And he continues: "No doubt the reason why the old 'law of causality' has so long continued to pervade the books of philosophers is simply that the idea of a function is unfamiliar to most of them, and therefore they seek an unduly simplified statement." [7]

One can agree with Russell that "the law of causality," whatever that means, has no place in science proper but is a typical philosophers' construction. Russell's denunciation of the very notion of cause is more controversial. His words seem to suggest that this notion is a prescientific ancestor of the scientific concept of a function.

It has been argued against Russell that, even though the words "cause" and "effect" and other elements of causal *terminology* are not prominent in the advanced theoretical sciences, causal ideas and causal thinking are not as outmoded as the shift in terminology, *e.g.* from speaking about "causal" to speaking about "functional" relationship, may suggest. As Ernest Nagel observes, the notion of cause "not only crops up in everyday speech, and in investigations into human affairs by economists, social psychologists, and historians, it is also pervasive in the accounts natural scientists give of their laboratory procedures, as well as in the interpretations offered by many theoretical physicists of their mathematical formalism." [8] Another prominent contemporary philosopher of science, Patrick Suppes, goes further still and says: "Contrary to the days when Russell wrote this essay the words 'causality' and 'cause' are commonly and widely used by physicists in their most advanced work." [9]

This last may nevertheless be an exaggeration. In trying to assess the importance of causation to science it is wise to remember that the word "cause," and causal terms generally, are used with a multitude of meanings. Not only are "causes" in human affairs very different from "causes" of natural events, but within the natural sciences as well causality is not a homogeneous category. The notion of cause which I will be discussing in this chapter is essentially tied to the idea of action and therefore, as a scientific notion, to the idea of experiment. It figures importantly, I think, in "the accounts natural scientists give of their laboratory procedures." But I am less certain whether this is what is involved "in the interpretations offered by many theoretical physicists of their mathematical formalism."

Causality and Causal Explanation

The reason why I nevertheless want to give a basic priority to this "actionist" or "experimentalist" notion of cause, is that, in addition to holding an important place in the experimental natural sciences, it seems largely to figure as a prototype for the idea of cause in the discussions of philosophers about universal causation, determinism *versus* freedom, interaction of body and mind, *etc.* I sympathize, however, with those who, like Russell or Norman Campbell,[10] have felt that *this* notion of cause is not so important in theoretically advanced sciences "such as gravitational astronomy" and who think that in them causal talk can profitably be replaced by talk about various functional relations. But whether or not this attitude is justified, the fact remains that causal thinking, as such, has not been exorcised from science—and that therefore the philosophical problems about causation continue to be central to the philosophy of science. Their seriousness is felt particularly keenly in the theory of scientific explanation.

The covering law model was originally thought of as a generalization of ideas associated with causal explanation.[11] The specific problems about causation seemed to many to have lost their urgency because of this widening of the conceptual horizon—just as Russell had thought that causation had become philosophically uninteresting because it might be subsumed under the broader category of functional relationship. But this is a mistake.

As we have already seen (Ch. I, Sect. 8), the notion of law which is involved in the subsumptive explanation model is itself problematic. Recent discussion of these problems has brought to the fore the modal ideas of natural necessity and nomic connection. These ideas in turn are closely associated with the ideas of cause and effect, so much so that one could conveniently group them all under the general head of causation. If one insists that the covering law model has explicative force only when the laws involved in it express (nonlogical) nomic connections, this would be tantamount to saying that explanation conforming to the covering law model and causal explanation are, substantially, the same thing. And this would at once turn the problematics associated with the hempelian model of explanation into a modern form of the problem of causation.[12]

2. Russell suggested that the place of the notion of cause in the philosophy of science be taken over by the notion of a function. There is another notion besides that of a function for which a similar claim could be made. This is the concept of *condition*. The discussion of cause and effect which I shall conduct here will be in terms of conditionship, and *not* of functional relationship.

One is used to distinguishing between necessary and sufficient conditions. Other condition concepts may also be defined: contributory conditions, substitutable requirements, *etc*. For the present purposes, however, these "minor" condition concepts will not be needed.[13]

The statement that the generic [14] phenomenon (state, event) p is a sufficient condition of q can, for purposes of a first approximation, be explained as follows: Whenever p is, q will be there too; the presence (occurrence) of p suffices to ensure the presence (occurrence) of q. That p is a necessary condition of q means that whenever q is, p has to be there too, *i.e.* the presence (occurrence) of q requires or presupposes the presence (occurrence) of p.

If p can be "manipulated," *i.e.* produced or prevented "at will" ("experimentally"), then, by producing p, we can also bring about anything of which it is a sufficient condition, and by removing or preventing p we can ensure that anything of which p is a necessary condition does *not* occur.

A phenomenon can be a necessary *and* sufficient condition of some other phenomenon. A phenomenon may have several sufficient or several necessary conditions. A condition can also be complex, *i.e.* a truth-functional compound of some generic phenomena. With regard to complexity and plurality of conditions the following asymmetries between the various kinds of condition must be noted.

A complex sufficient condition is a *conjunction* of phenomena. Maybe p by itself is not sufficient to guarantee that r will be, nor is q by itself sufficient for this. But if p and q occur together, r is sure to be there too. A complex necessary condition again is a *disjunction*. Maybe p does not require the presence of q (unconditionally), nor the presence of r (unconditionally); but p may nevertheless require that at least one of the two, q or r, be present.

Disjunctive sufficient conditions may be "resolved" into a plurality of sufficient conditions. If p or q is sufficient for r, then p by itself is sufficient and so is q by itself. Conjunctive necessary conditions may be similarly "resolved." If p and q is necessary for r, then p by itself is necessary and also q by itself.

These "asymmetries" of the condition concepts can be interestingly exploited in inductive logic.[15]

In terms of conditions one can distinguish a variety of causal factors which, when speaking vaguely of "cause" and "effect," are difficult, or even impossible, to separate.[16] Condition concepts are also helpful for making clearer the philosophers' ideas of (universal) Determinism and of the (universal) Law of Causation. I therefore find it surprising that the theory of condition concepts and its applications has remained relatively little developed and studied. In logic textbooks it is seldom even mentioned. Yet it seems to me eminently well suited as a propedeutics to logic and the methodology of science.

The usefulness of condition concepts is not in conflict with the fact that they also provoke problems. The problems may be said to concern the "place" of condition concepts in logic. Here two principal views confront each other. One places the condition concepts within quantification theory. In a logical language which employs names of individuals and predicates, the universal implication (x) $(Px \rightarrow Qx)$ would then be the "groundform" of conditionship relations. In a poorer language which employs only propositional variables, conditionship relations could be formulated, *e.g.*, as tense-logical statements, their "groundform" now being "whenever p then q," or in symbols: $\wedge (p \rightarrow q)$.

The view that condition concepts are *quantificational* ideas could also be called an *extensionalist* view of them. The alternative view I shall call *intensionalist*. According to this view, condition concepts are essentially *modal* ideas, and the "groundform" of a conditionship relation that of a strict implication, $N(p \rightarrow q)$.[17]

Perhaps one can regard quantification concepts as "philosophically" relatively unproblematic. An extensionalist view of conditionship relations might not, therefore, be connected with internal philosophical complications. The shortcomings of this view, as I see them, are "external." They consist in the fact that it is questionable whether this view can account *adequately* for conditionship. An adequate account, some may think, can only be given in modal terms. But modal concepts again are notoriously loaded with difficulties of a "philosophical" nature. Therefore an intensionalist view of conditionship relations will have to pay for its external adequacy with internal philosophical complications. These complications are largely the same as those which beset the idea of a *nomic,* or "lawlike," connection and which have been introduced into analytical philosophy principally by way of the problem of counterfactual conditionals. (See Ch. I, Sect. 8.)

The analysis of causal ideas by means of condition concepts neither evades nor solves the philosophical problems connected with causation or with the idea of natural law. But it is a useful way of presenting these problems more clearly.

3. Whether one takes an extensionalist or an intensionalist view of relations of conditionship, any attempt to analyze causality in terms of conditions has to face the following problem:

From the preliminary explanations we gave of the notions of sufficient and necessary conditions it follows that p is a sufficient condition of q if, and only if, q is a necessary condition of p. Thus if rainfall is a sufficient condition of the ground becoming wet, the ground becoming wet is a necessary condition of rainfall. Similarly, if the presence of oxygen in the environment is a necessary condition of the existence of higher forms of organic life, the existence of life is a sufficient condition of oxygen. As far as mere conditionship relations are concerned, these symmetries are quite in order, I should say. But as far as causality is concerned, they strike us as absurd. As the second example shows, the oddity is not that we attribute a causal role to a factor which is "only" necessary but not sufficient for something. The oddity springs from the fact that our explanations of the two types of condition blur an implicitly acknowledged *asymmetry* between conditioning or *cause*-factors on the one hand and conditioned or *effect*-factors on the other. If p is a cause-factor in relation to q, and q therefore an effect-factor in relation to p, we do not, or at least not normally, think of q as a cause-factor relative to p or of p as an effect-factor relative to q. (I say "cause-factors" and not "causes" in order to avoid an implicit identification here of "cause" with "sufficient condition.")

I shall refer to this problem as the problem of Asymmetry of Cause and Effect.

One could try to solve the problem by suggesting that the asymmetry in question simply reflects the asymmetry of temporal relationships. The occurrence of a cause-factor, one could argue, must precede in time the occurrence of a correlated effect-factor. The relation of temporal precedence is asymmetrical. If an occurrence of p precedes an occurrence of q in time, then *this* occurrence of q does not precede *that* occurrence of p. But it may, of course, happen that another occurrence of q precedes (that one or) another occurrence of p in time. Since p and q are generic phenomena, their temporal asymmetry, when they are related as cause to effect, must be an asymmetry of individual occurrences of the factors. (See below, Sect. 10.)

The question of the temporal relation of cause and effect gives rise to a number of problems. If the cause and the effect are phenomena which endure over a period of time, we must admit the possibility that the cause may outlast the effect. The temporal precedence of the cause would then consist in the fact that the cause comes into being before the effect. A more problematic question is whether there can be a lapse of time between the passing out of existence of a cause and the coming into being of the effect, or whether cause and effect must be, somehow, temporally contiguous.

An alternative to the view that the cause must precede the effect would be the view that the effect cannot precede the cause. This would allow for the possibility that a cause can (begin to) occur simultaneously with an effect of it. The relation of simultaneity, however, is symmetrical. If therefore cause and effect *can be* simultaneous, we must either abandon the view that the causal relation is *always* asymmetrical, or look for the ground of the asymmetry in something other than time.

It may even be wondered whether the effect may not sometimes occur, or begin to occur, before the cause. The possibility of "retroactive causation" has to be taken seriously, as I hope to be able to show later.

I shall not consider the problems of time and causation in any detail here.[18] My chief reason is that, in my opinion, the asymmetry of the causal relation, the separation of cause- from effect-factors, cannot be accounted for in terms of temporal relationships alone. The root of the asymmetry lies elsewhere.

To say this, however, is not to deny that time is an essential ingredient in the logical analysis of causation.

4. I shall next present the formal-logical apparatus which is presupposed in the present investigation. It is extremely simple.

Consider a set of logically independent generic states of affairs $p_1, p_2, \ldots$. Examples of such states of affairs could be that the sun is shining or that a certain door is open. I shall not further elucidate the notion of a state of affairs. It is not necessary for our purposes to think of the states as of something "static"; processes such as rainfall may also here be regarded as "states of affairs."

That the states are generic shall mean that they may obtain, or not, on given occasions—and thus obtain, and not obtain, repeatedly. I shall regard it as essential to all states which may enter into causal or other nomic connections with each other that they are in this sense generic. An occasion may also be called a location in space and/or time. Here we shall pay attention only to the temporal dimension of occasions.[19]

That the states are logically independent, finally, shall mean that it is *logically* possible for them, on any given occasion, to obtain or not obtain in any combination. If the number of states in the set is finite and equal to n, the number of such possible combinations is 2^n. Any one of these combinations will be said to constitute a *total state* or *possible world*. The term *state-description* has become current for the conjunction (the order of the conjuncts being irrelevant) of sentences and/or their negations, describing the states which are the "atoms" or "elements" of such a possible world.

The set of states which we are considering I shall also call a *state-space*. In the formal considerations which we are conducting here it will be assumed throughout that the state-spaces are finite.

Assume that the total state of the world on a given occasion can be completely described by stating for any given member of some state-space, whether or not this member obtains on that occasion. A world which satisfies this condition might be called a *Tractatus*-world. It is the kind of world which Wittgenstein envisaged in the *Tractatus*. It is a species of a more general conception of how the world is constituted. We can call this general conception *logical atomism*.

Is "the world," *i.e.* the world in which we are actually placed, a *Tractatus*-world or a world of logico-atomistic structure? This is a deep and difficult metaphysical question, and I do not know how to answer it. (The fact that a *Tractatus*-world is "narrow," *i.e.* that a great many familiar and important things remain outside its confines, is no decisive objection to this view of what the *world* is.) But independently of how we may answer the metaphysical question, it is an undeniable fact that

44

as a simplified *model* of a world, Wittgenstein's conception in the *Tractatus* is both interesting in itself and useful as a tool for a great many purposes in the philosophy of logic and of science. Here I shall employ this model throughout. This means, in particular, that states of affairs are the sole "ontological building-bricks" of the worlds we study. We shall not penetrate the inner structure of these bricks. Things, properties, and relations are ontological entities which fall outside the formal-logical frame of our investigations.

The basis of our logical formalism is "classical," two-valued Propositional Logic (PL). I shall assume that this fragment of logic is familiar to the reader; a presentation of it can be found in any textbook of elementary logic.

On this basis we erect a (rudimentary) tense-logic [20] as follows:

To the vocabulary of PL we add a new symbol T. It is a binary connective. The expression "pTq" can be read: "(now) the state p obtains *and next, viz.* on the next occasion, the state q obtains." The symbols to the left and right of T can also be compounds of variables and truth-connectives. Of particular interest is the case when they are state-descriptions. The whole expression then says that the world is now in a certain total state and on the next occasion in a certain total state, the same or a different one as the case may be.

The expressions to the left and the right of T may also themselves contain the symbol T. In this way we can construct chains of the form $-T(-T(-T \ldots)) \ldots$ which describe states which successively, *i.e.* on the various occasions over a finite period of time, obtain in the world. The case where the expressions occupying the places marked "$-$" are state-descriptions is of special interest. A chain of this character will be called a (fragment of the) *history* of the world. The word "history" has a useful ambiguity; it can mean both the succession of total states of the world and the description of (expressions depicting) this succession.

Explanation and Understanding

We obtain a "logic" of this connective T, if to the axioms of PL we add the following four axioms:

T1. $(pvqTrvs) \longleftrightarrow (pTr) \text{ v } (pTs) \text{ v } (qTr) \text{ v } (qTs)$

T2. $(pTq)\&(pTr) \rightarrow (pTq\&r)$

T3. $p \longleftrightarrow (pTqv\sim q)$

T4. $\sim(pTq\&\sim q)$

and to the rules of inference of PL add a rule to the effect that provably equivalent expressions are intersubstitutable (Rule of Extensionality).

If the number of possible total states of the world (on a given occasion) is 2^n, the number of possible histories of the world on m successive occasions is 2^{mn}. It is convenient to say that n measures the "width" of the world and that m measures the length of its history. The disjunction of the 2^{mn} different possible histories we shall call a *T-tautology* or "tautologous history." It tells us all the possible ways in which the world may change or remain unchanged in its singular features, when "time passes" from a first occasion to an m:th, without restricting the actual course of events in any way whatsoever. It thus says *nothing at all* about this history.

The notion of a T-tautology gives us a criterion of *logical truth* for the calculus of the connective T. It can be shown that those and only those formulas are provable in the calculus which are (provably equivalent with) T-tautologies. This means that the logic of T is *semantically complete*. It is also decidable; for any given formula we can tell whether or not it is (provably equivalent with) a T-tautology.

As should be obvious from the above explanations and from the structure of the formalism (particularly axiom T2), our tense-logic treats time as a *discrete* medium, a linear flow of countable successive occasions (moments, points in time). Again, as in the case of our assumption of logical atomism, one can ask whether time "really" has a discrete build. Must we not think of time as being at least "dense," *i.e.* such that between any two moments in time there is always a third? Or should we even think of it as continuous? We need not stop to discuss these questions here. As a simplified

46

model of the temporal succession of states of the world, the logic of the connective T is sufficient for present purposes.

Be it noted in passing that by the "simplicity" of the model I mean the logical primitiveness of its conceptual set-up. When, in science, causal relationships are formulated as functional dependencies between variables and when the functions are handled in mathematical calculations, it may be much simpler to treat time as continuous than to regard it as progressing in discrete steps. The view of the laws of nature as ideally a system of differential equations is allied with an idea of the continuity of time and space. Logically, however, this is a highly sophisticated and complex conception, and its relation to "reality" is not easy to determine. The idea of continuity can perhaps be called an "idealization" smoothing the rough surface of reality.

One can embellish the calculus of the connective T with a temporal quantifier, *e.g.* the concept "always" ("whenever"). If we symbolize "always" by $\wedge$, we can define "never" through the complex symbol $\wedge \sim$, and "sometimes" through $\sim \wedge \sim$. If we add $\wedge$ to the vocabulary of the T-calculus, we can express in our logical language such statements as, "Whenever p is the case, q will be the case on the next occasion." The symbolic expression for this is $\wedge (p \to (pTq))$. The axiomatics and metalogic (questions of completeness, decidability, *etc.*) of this quantified logic of discrete time need not be discussed here.[21]

The next, and last, conceptual ingredient which we add to our formalism is an operator M. This stands for the notion of possibility. We can then define impossibility through $\sim M$ and necessity through $\sim M \sim$. The axiomatics of the required modal logic should be *at least* as strong as the system constituted by PL, the Rule of Extensionality, and the following axioms:

M1. $M(pvq) \longleftrightarrow MpvMq$

M2. $p \to Mp$

M3. $\sim M(p \& \sim p)$

We shall not here prove theorems on an axiomatic basis, nor even try to express the results of our arguments in the symbolic language of the PL $+ T + \wedge + M$ calculus. The proper formalization of the logic of conditions and of what I propose to call causal analysis is still largely an open problem which I hope will be tackled and solved in due course. Here we provide at most only the ingredients for a solution.

Instead of formal developments within the calculus I shall employ a quasi-formal method of exposition and illustration by means of simple topological figures (trees). Let circles represent *total states* of the world "composed" of some n "elementary" states. Progressions from the left to the right of circles connected by lines shall represent *histories*. If a circle is connected with more than one circle to its immediate right, these latter circles represent alternative *possible* total states of the world subsequent to the state represented by the first circle.

The figure does not show anything about the "inner structure" of the total states (possible worlds) in terms of the n elements. It does not even show whether two circles represent the same or different total states. We shall adopt the convention that the alternative possibilities immediately after any given state shall all be different. (Otherwise we should sometimes have an entirely pointless multiplication of circles in the figure.) We shall also adopt the convention that the horizontal line of circles at the top (see *e.g.* the illustration on p. 50) represents the *actual* course of the world's history over a given stretch of occasions. Under this "surface of reality" are the "depths of alternative possibilities."

The picture allows us to study the "freedom of movement" which the world has, or would have had, at each stage in its history. This freedom can be greater or lesser at the various stages. It can be completely missing, in which case a given progression from a circle to another on its immediate right has no alternative. Or the world's freedom can be boundless. Then the world can change, in one step, from what it happens to be to any one of the 2^n worlds which may be composed of the same elements. If m signifies the number of alternative developments at a given stage in the world's history, we can use the fraction $\dfrac{m-1}{2^n-1}$ as a measure of the world's degree of freedom of development at this stage. When m has the minimum value 1, this degree is 0. The world's development from this stage to the next, the course of history at this point, is completely *determined*. When m has the maximum value 2^n, the degree of freedom is 1. The course of the world's history is now completely *indeterminate*.

I shall call a fragment of the history of a world such as we have just described, a *system*. A system, in this sense, is defined through a state-space, an initial state, a number of stages of development, and a set of alternative moves for each stage.

A given system can be enlarged. This may happen in two ways. The number of its stages of development can be extended, backward in time beyond the original initial state or forward in time beyond the original end-stage. Another extension is through the inclusion of new elements in the original state-space. An extension of the first type is reflected in the topological tree in a prolongation and possibly also multiplication of its branches. The second type of extension affects the form of the tree through a possible "split" of its nodes (and consequent multiplication of its branches). For example: If p was not originally in the state-space of the figure on p. 50, but is later included, the total state b, say, may be "split" into two, *viz.* $b\&p$ and $b\&\sim p$. But whether it actually will split like this depends upon the system's possibilities of development. Perhaps only $b\&p$, but not $b\&\sim p$ is possible after a. Then there will be no split at b. Similar arguments apply to all the other circles in the picture.

This use of "system" is not easily identifiable with any common or current use of the term.[22] But it is certainly related to several of its familiar uses.

An example of a system in our sense would be the putting into effect of a decision and calculating the subsequent possible developments over a limited period of time—the alternatives perhaps reflecting alternative reactions of affected agents to the consequences of the decision.[23] The activity called *planning* is something which normally approximates to such considerations about "systems" in our sense. Another example would be the observation, within a physically separated region in space, of a sequence of changes, say in states of temperature, humidity, air pressure, movements or chemical composition of its parts, *etc.* Scientific *experimentation* often takes place with or within systems of this nature; we shall later try to describe wherein the activist component of "making experiments" consists.

5. The presentation of systems in the form of topological trees which are fragments of a world's (possible) history offers a good starting point for a description of the activity which I propose to call *causal analysis.*

Consider the following picture of a system:

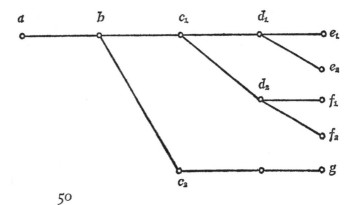

Causality and Causal Explanation

This system has actually passed through five stages, from a to e_1. Consider its end-state e_1. We want to investigate the "causes" of the origin and composition of this particular end-state. We ask, for example, whether the system's passing through d_1 at the fourth stage was a sufficient condition of its ending in the state e_1. The answer is plainly negative. For, after d_1 the end-state *could* also have been e_2. (It follows from our conventions of presentation that e_1 and e_2 are different total states of the system. See above, p. 48.)

Next we ask whether the system's passing through d_1 at its fourth stage of development was a necessary condition of its ending in the state e_1. In order to answer this question, we must consider the composition of all the other possible penultimate states of the system and of the possible end-states after them. If an end-state identical with e_1 materializes only after states identical with d_1, then the answer to the question is affirmative; otherwise it is negative.

It should be noted that the full meaning of the question whether d_1 is a certain sort of condition of the system's end-state e_1 is the following: Is the fact that the system at its fourth stage is in a state *generically identical* with d_1, i.e. has the same composition as d_1 in terms of the elements of the state-space under consideration, a condition of that sort of an end-state generically identical with e_1?

The questions to which the causal analysis gives an answer can be varied in a number of ways. I shall not try to treat the subject exhaustively or systematically here, but only to consider a few more special cases. Instead of inquiring into the causal antecedents of the end-state *as a whole*, we may be interested in some special feature of it, *i.e.* in "elementary" states such as p or q. Assume that p is a conjunct in e_1. Is d_1 at the fourth stage a sufficient condition of the occurrence of p in the end-state? If p occurs in every possible end-state of the system which originates from (d_1, or from) a penultimate state identical with d_1, the answer is affirmative; otherwise it is negative.

Let the next question be whether d_1 was a necessary condition of the occurrence of p in the end-state. If p occurs only in such possible end-states of the system which originate from a penultimate state identical with d_1, *i.e.* if p is missing from every end-state after a penultimate state which is different in composition from d_1, then the answer is affirmative; otherwise it is negative.

We extend this search for "causes" of a given state or feature of a state backwards in time. We then note something which proves to be of fundamental importance to the metaphysics of causation:

The fact that a certain state at a certain stage in the history of a system is *not* a *necessary* condition of the system's end-state (or of some feature of the end-state) is compatible with the possibility that some state at an earlier stage *is* such a condition. For example: Let it be that d_1 at the fourth stage is *not* a necessary condition of the occurrence of p in e_1, say because p occurs in f_1, too. In spite of this, c_1 at the third stage may be necessary for the appearance of p in e_1. This would actually be the case, if p does not occur in g.

On the other hand, the fact that a certain state at a certain stage is *not* a *sufficient* condition of the system's end-state (or of some feature in it) entails that no state at an earlier stage is such a condition. For example: If d_1 is not a sufficient condition for p in e_1—say because p does not appear in e_2—then c_1 cannot be this either.

Causal analysis need not proceed from a given state of a system towards the past. It can also proceed towards the future. Assuming parallelism between the irreversibility of time on the one hand and the asymmetry of the causal relation on the other, causal analysis of the first type is essentially a tracing of causes of given effects, whereas analysis of the second type traces the effects of given causes. The posterior states which are related causally to a given state are often also called its "consequences." (Cf. Ch. III, Sect. 2.)

Causal analysis which proceeds in direction towards the future will not be treated separately here.

Next let us consider a fragment only of the system pictured on p. 50, say the fragment beginning with the state c_1. Assume that the state p occurs in e_1 but not in f_1 or f_2. (Whether it occurs or not in e_2 is immaterial.) Within the smaller system now under consideration a necessary condition of p's occurring in the end-state is then that the penultimate state is identical with d_1. But it does not follow that the same is true of the bigger system. If p is a feature of the possible end-state g and if the state immediately preceding it is different from d_1 (which we are free to imagine), then the above conditionship relation does not hold for the bigger system.

Similarly for relations of sufficient conditionship. If p occurs in e_1 and e_2 then, in the fragment system, the penultimate state d_1 is a sufficient condition of the appearance of p in the end-state. But if p is not a feature of g and the state immediately preceding g is identical with d_1, then this conditionship relation is not valid in the bigger system.

It is easy to see that, if a conditionship relation holds in the bigger system, then it also necessarily holds in the smaller system which is a fragment of it, but not conversely.[24]

Assume, as before, that in the system beginning with c_1 a penultimate state identical with d_1 is a necessary condition of an end-state containing p, but that this does not hold true for the system beginning with a. Since the system beginning with c_1 is a fragment of the system beginning with a, the conditionship relation in question can be said to hold in the following *relative* [25] sense within the bigger system too: *If the bigger system evolves from its initial state a through b to c_1, then* it is necessary that it should go through d_1 if it is to end in a state containing *p*. Here the antecedent lays down a sufficient condition of the (obtaining of the) relationship of necessary condition expressed in the consequent.[26]

If a conditionship relation is true of a system as a whole, and not only of some fragment of it, then this conditionship is not, in its turn, conditioned by any developments within the system. No matter which alternatives the system "chooses" in the course of its development, the appearance of, say, *F* at the *m*:th stage is related in a specified way to the appearance of, say, *G* at the *n*:th stage. But the conditionship in question is still *relative to the system.*[27]

There are several senses in which a system, when it is instantiated, can be said to be *closed* to causal influences from outside the system.[28] One sense is that no state (or feature of a state) at any stage in the system has an *antecedent sufficient condition* occurring outside the system. Since the word "cause" is quite commonly used to refer to something which is a sufficient condition of something else, I think that this sense of closedness to causal influences is what we very often contemplate when we speak of a certain chain of successive states as forming a "closed system." I shall henceforward use the term *a closed system* in this sense throughout.

This notion of a closed system can be *relativized* in a variety of ways. One relativization of it is when the system is closed with regard to *some* though not necessarily *all* of its states, *i.e.* when some of its states do not have outside antecedent sufficient conditions although some others of its states may have such conditions.

Causality and Causal Explanation

6. Causal *analysis* should be distinguished from causal *explanation*. In the former we are given a system and try to discover conditionship relations within it. In the latter we are given an individual occurrence of some generic phenomenon (event, process, state) and look for a system within which this (generic) phenomenon, the *explanandum*, may become correlated with another through some conditionship relation.

One can further distinguish kinds or types of causal explanation depending on the nature of the conditionship relation involved and/or the place of the conditionship relation in the system as a whole. I shall here consider only a few prototype cases.

i. Given a total state c, composed of some elementary states $p_1 \ldots p_n$. Why did c happen (come about)? The explanation could be that c occurred after another total state b composed of the same elementary states and that the occurrence of b is a sufficient condition of the occurrence of c. If this is a valid explanation, we have a system of extremely simple structure; an initial state b followed, without alternatives, by an end-state c.

ii. Given a total state c. Why did *this* state materialize and not, *e.g.*, another state c' which we also consider possible? That we consider c' a possible alternative to c must be understood relative to the position of the states in a history. It means, strictly speaking, that after the total state b, known to have preceded c, c' was also possible. The topological picture of the system is

In order to answer the question why c occurred, we must extend this system with regard either to its temporal dimension or to its state-space. We shall consider the second possibility first. We discover, for example, that on the occasion when b materialized there obtained also a state p which is not an element of the original state-space. When p is included in the state-space and the states are redescribed, we obtain, say, this picture of a (fragment of a) system:

In answer to our original question we can now say that c materialized, and not c', because the occurrence of p under the circumstances b is a sufficient condition of the occurrence of the end-state c (whether or not p remains in the world).

When an explanation is of this type, we very often say that p is the "cause" of c. Then it should be observed, however, that the "cause" here need be neither a sufficient nor a necessary condition of the effect. The "cause" is a factor which, when "added" to a given constellation of circumstances, the total state b, turns this constellation into a sufficient condition of something else. Perhaps one could, adopting a term suggested by Ernest Nagel, call p a "contingent sufficient condition." One could also call it a "relative" condition.[29]

iii. The splitting of the state b in the case just described led to the discovery of a (relative) sufficient condition of the end-state. It could also have led to the discovery of a (relative) necessary condition. We find, *e.g.*, that only when the state b materializes with the additional feature p is it followed by the end-state c. Had it not been for the occurrence of p in b, c

would *not* have come about. This is not to say that *c* will come about whenever *p* is added to *b*. The topological figure corresponding to this type of a causal explanation could look like this

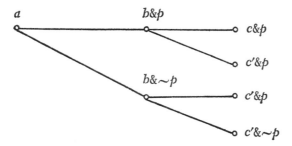

If we change this last picture slightly, so that the second circle from the top in the extreme right-hand column is made to represent the state $c\&\sim p$, then the occurrence of *p* in *b* is, in the relative sense, both necessary *and* sufficient for *c*. We have then succeeded in detecting in the state preceding the *explanandum* a feature whose absence from this state (everything else in it being unchanged) would have prevented the *explanandum* from materializing, and whose presence in this state (with the rest of it) guarantees the materialization of the *explanandum*.

iv. We go back to the question raised in *ii.* One way of answering it, we said, is through an extension of the fragment

in time. This happens as follows: We observe that the state following *after* the *explanandum c* is the state *d*; *c*, we think, is a *necessary* condition of this state. The state *d* materialized—but had it not been for *c*, *d* would not have come about; *c* was needed to make *d* possible, one could say. We are not here interested in explaining *d*. We take its occurrence for granted. In the light of this the "purpose," so to say, of *c* was to make *d* possible; *c*, as it were, is there "for the sake of" *d*. The figure corresponding to this explanation could be, *e.g.*:

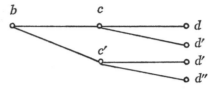

This bears a certain resemblance to the figure under *iii*. An important difference is that the *explanandum* is in a different relative position in the two schemas.

An explanation of type *iv* I shall call *quasi-teleological*.

Explanations of the types *i* and *ii* answer questions as to *why* something was or became *necessary*; explanations of the types *iii* and *iv* again show *how* something was or became *possible*. In explanations of the *Why necessary?* type sufficient conditions are crucial; in explanations of the *How possible?* type, necessary conditions.[30]

Explanations of the first two types can be used for predictions. When the sufficient condition is there, or the relative sufficient condition has been fitted into its appropriate frame, we can predict the effect, *i.e.* the recurrence of the *explanandum* of our explanation.

Explanations of the last two types *cannot* be used for predicting new occurrences of the *explanandum*. (It is thus, for this reason alone, a mistake to think that a causal explanation, or a scientific explanation generally, is necessarily equivalent to a mechanism for predicting the phenomena explained; yet this mistake is not infrequently made.)[31] But they can be used for making what could aptly be called *retrodictions*. From the fact that a phenomenon is known to have occurred, we can infer back in time that its antecedent necessary conditions must also have occurred, in the past. And by "looking into the past" we may find traces of them (in the present). This mechanism of testing or verification will not be investigated further here. Prediction and retrodiction are, in fact, more unlike each other than is sometimes thought.

In an "oblique" manner, however, explanations of the *How possible?* type too can be used for predictions. If we know the necessary conditions of a phenomenon we can, by suppressing them or by simply observing that they are absent, predict that the phenomenon in question will *not* occur.

Explanations with predictive power are of paramount importance in the experimental sciences. Retrodictive explanations again are prominent in sciences which, like cosmogony, geology, and the theory of evolution, search into the history (development) of natural events and processes.

Explanations of the kind I call quasi-teleological have received relatively little attention from methodologists and philosophers of science.[32] They have not been distinguished from teleological explanations proper, and thus their distinctive *causal* character, *i.e.* their dependence on nomic connections between phenomena, has largely gone unrecognized. I think that quasi-teleological explanations in terms of consequents of the phenomenon to be explained play a great role in the biological sciences.[33] They may be regarded as characteristic of those sciences in much the same way as causal explanations in terms of antecedents are characteristic of the sciences of inorganic nature. Functional explanations in biology usually seem to be of the type here called quasi-teleological. The behavior of a living body or of a machine which is explained quasi-teleologically can also be called *purposeful.* It is purposeful in the sense of being needed for the performance of functions characteristic of certain systems. Behavior and other processes which are in this sense purposeful must be distinguished from behavior which is *purposive* in the sense of intentionally aiming at ends. Various "vitalistic" opinions in the philosophy of biology are often guilty of a confusion between purposeful and purposive behavior.

7. How do we learn to "isolate" closed systems from their surroundings of external circumstances, and how do we get to know the possibilities of development inherent in a system?

In the succession of occasions we have repeatedly noted the occurrence of a certain state a. It has always, in our experience, been followed by a state b, this again sometimes by c_1 and sometimes by c_2, c_1 sometimes or always by ——, c_2 sometimes or always by ——, and so forth through a number of, say n, stages. In these successions of events we have, by the tools of causal analysis, been able to discern certain conditionship relations. But how do we know that the alternative possibilities of development, as familiar to us from the observations, really represent all the possibilities? Can continued *observation* of successions ever give us the required assurance here?

Consider a number of repeated occurrences of the initial state a. The state a always originates from some immediately preceding state. Assume now that there is a state α such that we feel confident, on the basis of past experience, that α *will not change* to the state a, unless *we change it* to a. And assume this is something (we know) we *can do*. These assumptions may seem extremely problematic. How can we be sure that α will not change to a "of itself," *i.e.* independently of our action? And how do we know *we* can change it? We need not deny that here are grave problems for a philosopher. But we must also admit the empirical fact that situations of the kind just described are familiar to us. I know (feel sure) that the window in front of me will not open "of itself," but that I can open it. I *may* be mistaken, of course. Surprising things happen in nature and unexpected disabilities sometimes befall a man. But on the whole such knowledge is reliable. If it were not, *action* would not be (commonly) possible—and, *a fortiori*, neither would the activity which we call scientific experimentation. For it is an essential feature of action that changes should happen of which we can say confidently that they would not have happened had it not been for our interference, and also that changes fail to take place of which we can confidently say that they would have occurred had we not prevented them.[34]

The assumption we are making is, be it observed, not an assumption about a causal conditionship relation. It is not assumed that the state α is a sufficient condition of not-a. Nor do we assume that changing α to a requires knowledge of sufficient conditions of a. Sometimes knowledge of such conditions plays an important part in our changing of the situation. But this is not always the case.

Now assume that we change α to a and watch what happens. Assume we find that the system goes through one of its hypothetically admitted moves from initial state to end-state.

The manipulation described makes possible a very powerful logical conclusion. It is that neither α nor any state which occurred *anterior* to α can be a *sufficient* condition of the initial state of the system as instantiated. A sufficient condition from the past can work only through an uninterrupted chain of successive sufficient conditions within the system, the initial state of which is that condition occurring in the past. But any such chain, if there is one, is interrupted at α. Because α, we assumed, will not change to a unless *we* change it.

61

The act of interference which we have been considering does not yet guarantee closedness for the "interior" of the system. There may occur some state (or feature of a state) in it of which α, or some state anterior to α, is a sufficient condition. How is this possibility to be excluded?

First it should be noted that, if there is such a (feature of a) state in the system, then there must exist an uninterrupted chain of sufficient conditions linking it with its "outside" sufficient condition in the bigger system initiated by the occurrence of that outside state. (See above p. 61.) So we need in fact consider only such (features of) states in the system of which the system's initial state is a sufficient condition. Assume there is such a state. For example, assume that p occurs in all the possible end-states of the system pictured on p. 50. Then the initial state a of the system is a sufficient condition of it. In order to eliminate the possibility that some state anterior to a is a sufficient condition of the appearance of p in every end-state of the system, it is enough to show that α is not such a sufficient condition. How is this done?

We do this by *refraining* from the action of changing α to a and by observing what happens then. We *let the world change* independently of our interference—which may of course mean that it does not change at all, but remains in a state identical with α. If, when this "untouched" world has passed through the five stages, corresponding (in time) to the stages from a to the end-state of our system, it does *not* exhibit the feature p, we can be sure that α is not a sufficient condition of the occurrence of p in the end-state of our system. If again it exhibits this feature, then we have to reckon with the possibility that α actually is such a condition and that the system is therefore not closed. No act of trying to "remove" p from the end-state could give us this assurance of closedness. Here we are dependent upon "the grace of nature."

Causality and Causal Explanation

The fact that the system can be put in motion by changing α to a does not, of course, rule out the possibility that a has one or several sufficient conditions which are alternatives to α. Let α' be such a condition. The system beginning with a can thus recur as a fragment of a bigger system beginning with α'. The question may be raised of whether or not the bigger system can occur closed. In order to find the answer, we look for a possibility of operating this bigger system by producing *its* initial state α' from some antecedent state.

Another possibility which is *not* ruled out by the act of changing α to a is that α itself or some state or states anterior to α are necessary conditions of a or of some of the states in the system after a. Of such anterior states we should say that they *make possible* the performance of the action of producing a (from α) or of bringing about something by producing a. These states can, but need not, be states which we can produce, if they are not there. (On the distinction between doing and bringing about see Sect. 8.)

It seems to be true generally that "outside" necessary conditions of states in a system which is experimentally reproducible are thought of as conditions of *performing the experiment* rather than as conditions of its *results*.

If we were compelled to "passive" observation only of successions of events, we should not be able to make sure that on an occasion when the initial state of a system materializes, there is not some sufficient condition in its past which is "responsible" for its occurrence. It is *only* the characteristic operation of "active" interference, of changing a state, which would otherwise *not* thus change, into the initial state of a system, that can give us this assurance.[35]

Our answer to the question of how we learn to isolate a fragment of a world's history to a closed system and get to know the possibilities (and necessities) which govern the developments inside a system is thus as follows: We learn this partly by repeatedly putting the system in motion through acts of producing its initial state and then watching ("passively") the successive stages of its development, and partly by comparing these successive stages with developments in systems originating from different initial states.

What we learn from the act of experimental interference and subsequent observation does not amount to a definitive verification either of the closed character of the system or of its possibilities of development. There are several reasons for this. If the system exhibits alternative developments, these will have to be learned through repeated experiments with varying results of observation. If there is very great variation in the results, and consequently very little predictability of the actual course of events on an individual realization of the system, our interest in studying it soon ceases and we have no confidence in the assertion that we know (all) its possibilities of development. Even when no alternatives to an observed regularity have yet been noted, we can never be completely sure that some will not one day be found.

8. In the idea of putting systems in motion the notions of action and of causation meet. This confrontation has deep roots in history, as language itself testifies.

It is natural to speak of the causes of phenomena as factors which "produce" or "bring about" their effects. The way a cause operates is often compared to the operation of an agent, who is held responsible for what he does. Some historians of ideas (Jaeger, Kelsen) maintain that the ancient Greeks modeled their idea of causation in nature by analogy with ideas from the realm of criminal law and distributive justice.[36] The cause brings about a disturbance of a state of equilibrium and is thus responsible for some evil or wrong in nature. This evil is then retributively corrected in accordance with nature's law. The Greek word for cause, *aitia*, also means guilt. The Latin *causa* was in origin a legal term.[37] It may be mentioned here that the Finnish word for cause, *syy*, has exactly the same double meaning as *aitia*. "Aetiology" is still used in medicine as a name for the science of causes of diseases, *i.e.* obnoxious disturbances of the natural state of the body. But it could also be another name of the theory and practice of investigations into causes generally.

These observations on language do not by themselves establish that there is a conceptual connection between the notions of cause and of action. Talk of causes as operating agents, responsible for their effects, is primarily analogical or metaphorical talk. When taken literally, it easily encourages superstitious beliefs in invisible "powers" behind the observable course of nature, and in their obscure designs. As man's insight into the causal connections and mechanisms of nature has grown and become more "scientific," we have gradually rid ourselves of these superstitions. Perhaps we can witness their last vestiges in the "vitalistic" ideas which still haunt the philosophy (or at least some philosophers) of biology. There can be little doubt that they will disappear as science progresses. In this respect cybernetics has meant a great step forward towards a scientific purification of our views of the life processes.

But observations about the purification of causal conceptions in science from traces of animism and magic are as little capable of proving that cause and action can become conceptually divorced as are etymological observations of proving that our concepts of cause and action are related. I would maintain that we cannot understand causation, nor the distinction between nomic connections and accidental uniformities of nature, without resorting to ideas about doing things and intentionally interfering with the course of nature.

In order to make my viewpoint clearer something more must be said here, and later, to elucidate the concept of human action.

It is convenient to distinguish between *doing* things and *bringing about* things, and therefore also between ability to do and ability to bring about. By *doing* certain things we bring about other things. For example, by opening a window we let fresh air into the room (bring about ventilation), or lower the temperature, or bring it about that a person in the room feels uncomfortable, starts to sneeze, and eventually catches a cold. What we thus bring about are the effects of our action. That which we do is the cause of those effects. The cause I shall also call the *result* and the effects the *consequences* of our action. Between the cause and the effects there is a conditionship relation of some sort. The opening of the window can, for example, be a sufficient condition of the dropping of the temperature given the present frame of prevailing circumstances. One of these circumstances is that the temperature in the room is higher than the outdoor temperature.[38]

Assume we brought about the ventilation of the room by opening the window, *i.e.* by doing something. Did we not also "bring about" the opening of the window? If we say that we brought about the opening of the window, this would normally indicate that we achieved this by doing something else, such as pressing a button and thus releasing a spring. But if we had to explain to somebody else *how* we opened the window, and said that we did this by first seizing the handle, then turning it clockwise, and finally pushing against the frame, then it would also be correct to say that we brought about the opening of the window by successively doing these things. The pushing was, under the circumstances, a sufficient condition of the window opening, but the turning of the handle was a necessary condition of creating the circumstances which made pushing sufficient to achieve the opening.

Suppose someone asked how I turned the handle, and I answer that I seized it with my right hand and turned the hand clockwise. Here again it would be correct to say that I brought about the turning of the handle by performing those actions. But if someone were to ask how I turned my hand, it would *not* be correct to say that I brought this about by contracting and relaxing a particular group of muscles. For, unless I happen to have a special knowledge of anatomy, I do not know which muscles these are nor how to contract them—except by turning my hand.

The thing done is the result of an action; the thing brought about is the consequence of an action. Primarily, the things done and brought about are changes (events). Changes are transitions from one state of affairs to another. The result (and also the consequences) can be identified with the change *or* with its end-state. For present purposes it is immaterial which alternative we choose. For reasons of simplicity I shall choose the latter. It should be observed that when the result is the obtaining of a state, it does not answer uniquely to the performance of an act. For example: the result of the act of opening a window is that a certain window is open. But the same state, *viz.* that a window is open, can also be a result of the act of preventing the window from closing. (And it can be the result of either of two different "negative" acts of forbearing to do things: of leaving the window open or of letting it change from closed to open.)

The connection between an action and its result is intrinsic, logical and not causal (extrinsic). If the result does not materialize, the action simply has not been performed. The result is an essential "part" of the action. It is a *bad* mistake to think of the act(ion) itself as a cause of its result.

The distinction between result and consequences is in an important sense *relative*. When I say that I ventilate the room by opening the window, the result of action here is that the window opens (is open). When I say that I open the window by turning the handle, *etc.*, the change in position of the handle, *etc.*, is the result, the change in position of the window the consequence. Such chains always and necessarily terminate in something I do, not *by doing* something else, but *simpliciter*. Actions of which it would not be true to say that they are performed by doing something else, I shall call *basic actions*.[39]

In the terminology of "systems," the performance of an action, whether basic or not, means the transition from a state preceding the initial state of a system to this initial state. The result is the initial state. The performance of an action is thus the putting in motion of a system.

In the limiting case, the system under consideration has only one stage. This happens when the result of the action is not related (by us) to anything else as a consequence.

Whenever we bring about something by doing something else, we presuppose the existence of a system which passes through at least two stages and within which a relation of sufficient conditionship between states can be discerned.

The idea that man, through his action, *can bring about* things is founded on the idea that sequences of events form closed systems, if not absolutely, then at least relative to some conditionship relation between their states. The identification and isolation of systems again rests on the idea that man *can do* things, as distinct from bringing them about, through a direct interference with the course of events (nature).

Causality and Causal Explanation

We perform actions. Can actions be done? There is a slight oddity about an affirmative answer. This is probably because saying that an action is done suggests that an action is the result of an action. I shall not stop to discuss whether this *cannot*, for conceptual reasons, be the case. If one makes a distinction between act and action and regards the latter as something which manifests itself "in the world" through an event or a state called its result and regards the former as something purely "inner," one could perhaps say that actions can be the results of acts, *e.g.* the action of opening the window can be a result of the act of deciding to do so. (It is significant that a decision is not called an action.)

Whether actions can properly be said to be done may be doubtful, but it certainly makes good sense to say that actions are sometimes "brought about." People are *made to do* things. How does this happen? For example, by commanding, or intimidating, or persuading, or requesting, or threatening agents. Actions thus brought about can be called consequences or effects of those actions which brought them about. But this is *not*, I maintain, a causal or nomic connection of the kind we are here investigating. It is a motivational mechanism and, as such, not causal but teleological. (See below, Ch. IV, Sect. 5.)

9. When we say that the cause brings about the effect, we do not mean that the cause *by doing something* brings this about. Thanks to the fact that *it happens*, the cause achieves this. (The verbs "achieve," "bring about," "produce," are all loaded with metaphors from the language of action.) But by *making* the cause *happen*, we achieve or bring about the same as the cause does by happening. To say that we cause effects is not to say that agents are causes. It means that we do things which then as causes produce effects, "act" or "operate" as causes.

Explanation and Understanding

I now propose the following way of distinguishing between cause and effect by means of the notion of action: p is a cause relative to q, and q an effect relative to p, if and only if by doing p we could bring about q or by suppressing p we could remove q or prevent it from happening. In the first case the cause-factor is a sufficient, in the second case it is a necessary condition of the effect-factor. The factors can become "relativized" to an environment of other factors. Then the cause is not "by itself," but only "under the circumstances," a sufficient or necessary condition of the effect. (Cf. above, Sect. 6.)

But is it true that we always think of the cause as something that can be done? The eruption of Vesuvius was the cause of the destruction of Pompeii. Man can through his action destroy cities, but he cannot, we think, make volcanoes erupt. Does this not prove that the cause-factor is not distinguished from the effect-factor by being in a certain sense capable of manipulation? The answer is negative. The eruption of a volcano and the destruction of a city are two very complex events. Within each of them a number of events or phases and causal connections between them may be distinguished. For example, that when a stone from high above hits a man on his head, it kills him. Or that the roof of a house will collapse under a given load. Or that a man cannot stand heat above a certain temperature. All these are causal connections with which we are familiar from experience and which are such that the cause-factor typically satisfies the requirement of manipulability.

Could one not argue against our position as follows: *If* it is true that p is always and invariably accompanied by q, then surely *it follows* that also in the cases when p is done (produced "at will") q will be there as well. So causality does not *rest on* an idea of doing things, but itself provides a basis for possible manipulation. To argue thus, however, is to beg the question. For consider what the assumption of universal concomitance of p and q amounts to. Either it just *so happens* that p is always succeeded by q and the causal or nomic character of the uniformity is never put to the test by doing p in a situation in which it would not "of itself" come about. (Perhaps p is something which we cannot do.) Then there is nothing which decides whether the truth of the general proposition is only accidental or whether it reflects a natural necessity. *Or* there have been such tests and they were successful. The assumption (hypothesis) that the concomitance of p and q has a nomic character contains *more* than just the assumption that their togetherness is invariable. It also contains the *counterfactual assumption* that on occasions when p, in fact, was not the case q would have accompanied it, had p been the case. The fact that it is a ground for counterfactual conditionals is what *marks* the connection as nomic. (Cf. Ch. I, Sect. 8.)

It is logically impossible to verify on any single occasion when p was (is) not there, what would have been the case, had p been there. But there is a way of coming "very close" to such a verification. It is this:

Assume that p is a state of affairs which, on some occasions at least, we can produce or suppress "at will." This presupposes that there are occasions on which p is not already there and, we feel confident, will not come to be (on the next occasion), unless *we* produce it. Assume there is such an occasion and that we produce p. We are then confident that had we not done this, the next occasion would have been one when p was *not* there. But in fact it is one when p *is* there. If then q too is there, we should regard this as a confirmation of the counterfactual conditional which we could have affirmed had we not

71

produced p, *viz.* that had p which was not there been there q would have been there too. This is as "near" as we can come to the verification of a counterfactual conditional.

The counterfactual conditional confirmed through the operation, be it observed, "rests" on another counterfactual conditional, *viz.* the one which says that p would not have been there had we not produced it. This counterfactual conditional is not a statement of a conditionship relation nor of a causal connection.

The above reasoning shows, I think, in which sense the idea of a causal or nomic relationship can be said to depend on the concept of action, *i.e.* on the factual conditions which make action *logically* possible.[40]

It is *established* that there is a causal connection between p and q when we have satisfied ourselves that, by manipulating the one factor, we can achieve or bring it about that the other is, or is not, there. We usually satisfy ourselves as to this by making experiments.

By "removing" p from a situation in which p occurs together with q and finding that q then vanishes as well, we aim at showing that p is a necessary condition of q. This has been established when we can confidently say: "We *can* make q vanish, *viz.* by removing p."

Similarly, we aim at showing that p is a (relative) sufficient condition of q by "introducing" p into a situation from which both p and q are missing, and finding that then q too comes about. The causal relation has become established when we can say: "We *can* produce q, *viz.* by producing p."

When we cannot interfere with p and q, we can nevertheless *assume* that there is a causal bond between them. This would be tantamount to assuming, *e.g.*, that *if we could* produce p as a result of action, we could also bring about q, *viz.* by producing *p*. But only through experiments could this assumption be tested.

What has been said here does not mean that causal laws, nomic connections, can be "conclusively verified." But it means that their confirmation is not a mere matter of repeated lucky observations. It is a matter of "putting the law to a test." That such test is successful (with a view to the truth of the law) means that we learn how to do things by doing other things (which we already know how to do), that our technical mastery of nature is increased. One could say that we can be as certain of the truth of causal laws as we can be of our abilities to do, and bring about, things.[41]

We may be mistaken in thinking that we *can do* things. Sometimes we have to concede that it was only "by chance" that *q* appeared when we did *p*; further experiments fail. Or we may have to limit our initial claim to a more or less vaguely conceived frame of "normal circumstances." When an assumed connection (law) fails to hold in an individual case, we need not drop the law, but can make the circumstances responsible for an accidental failure. Sometimes a hypothesis is formed that there was a "counteracting cause." This is an assumption to the effect that it might be possible to control (part of the) circumstances under which a law is tested. The truth of the law can in principle always be placed entirely in our hands. This fact is a source of the position called "conventionalism" (Ch. I, Sect. 8).

The thesis that the distinction between cause- and effect-factors goes back to the distinction between things done and things brought about through action does not mean that whenever a cause can be truly said to operate some agent is involved. Causation operates throughout the universe—also in spatial and temporal regions forever inaccessible to man. Causes do their

job whenever they happen, and whether they "just happen" or
we "make them happen" is accidental to their nature as causes.
But to think of a relation between events as causal is to think
of it under the aspect of (possible) action. It is therefore true,
but at the same time a little misleading to say that if p is
a (sufficient) cause of q, then if I could produce p I could
bring about q. For *that* p is the cause of q, I have endeavored
to say here, *means* that I could bring about q, if I could do
(so that) p.

No proof can decide, I think, which is the more basic concept, action or causation. One way of disputing my position
would be to maintain that action cannot be understood unless
causation is already intelligible. I shall not deny that this view
too could be sustained by weighty arguments.

10.   We can now tackle the problem of the *asymmetry* of the
causal relation (which we raised in Section 3). If p is the cause-
and q the effect-factor, then it will have to be the case either
that by doing p I could (can) bring about q or by doing $\sim p$ I
could (can) bring about $\sim q$. Is this relation asymmetrical?

Here it is important to keep in mind the distinction between
the generic factors, p, q, *etc.*, and their instantiations, occurrences on particular occasions. Consider the following simple
mechanism. There are two buttons in front of me. They are
so connected that by pressing down the button to the left, I
make the button to the right sink too, and *vice versa*. When I
release my finger, the buttons return to normal. This is a case
when by doing p I bring about q ($=$ that the button to the
right sinks down), and by doing q I bring about p ($=$ that the
button to the left sinks down).

For all its simplicity this is a difficult case. To say that here
p is the cause of q, but also q the cause of p, seems true. But

74

it would not follow that the causal relation is symmetrical. For, in the cases when by doing *p* we bring about *q*, it is *p* that is the cause and not *q*, and in the cases when by doing *q* we bring about *p*, it is *q* that is the cause and not *p*.

The cases when by doing *p* we bring about *q* are not, be it observed, cases when *p* occurs first and then *q*, nor are the cases when by doing *q* we bring about *p*, cases when *q* occurs before *p*. The example was so conceived that *p* and *q*, when they happen, occur simultaneously. So we cannot use *time* to distinguish the cases when *p* causes *q* from those when *q* causes *p*. How then shall we distinguish them? As far as I can see, the *only* way to do this is in terms of doing and bringing about. *In the cases* when I bring about *q* by doing *p*, *p* is the cause and not *q*; and *in the cases* when I bring about *p* by doing *q*, *q* is the cause and not *p*.[42]

It may, however, be doubted whether this attempt to distinguish between cause and effect here is entirely successful. A stone drops (no one dropped it), hits the button to the left (right), and both buttons sink under the pressure. The fact that the one button *was hit* by the stone caused the sinking of both buttons because of the way the buttons are connected. But would it be right to say in this case that the *sinking* of the button which happened to be hit caused the sinking of the other button?

In a similar manner I might say that by applying pressure (*e.g.* with my finger) to the button to the left (right) I make both buttons go down. Here again I view the *sinking* of the buttons as the effect of the *pressure* exerted by my finger on one of them. The result of the act of applying pressure is that pressure works on the buttons. As a consequence of (the result of) this act the buttons sink.

It seems that the application of the cause-effect distinction to two simultaneous events requires that there is some *basic* action, *i.e.* an action which we can do "directly" and not only by doing something else, the result of which is the one (but not the other) of the two events. Inasmuch as the pressing down of a button is not a basic action, we failed in the above example to make the distinction. I am therefore not certain whether genuine examples of "simultaneous causation" can be found.

We now change the example a little. When the button to the left is pressed, the one to the right sinks a second later; and vice versa. (When pressure is released, both buttons return to normal.) Here we have a temporal asymmetry in addition to the asymmetry between doing and bringing about. The two asymmetries, moreover, run parallel. The cases when q is brought about by doing p are all of them cases when p precedes q; and the cases when p is brought about by doing q are all of them cases when q precedes p. But *must* the two asymmetries necessarily be parallel?

The answer would be negative if we could find an instance where by doing something now one can bring it about that something happened in the past. I think that such instances might be found. The examples we are looking for are provided by the basic actions.

The result of a basic action may have necessary, and also sufficient, conditions in antecedent neural events (processes) regulating muscular activity. These neural events I cannot "do" by simply making *them* happen. But I can nevertheless bring them about, *viz.* by performing the basic action in question. What I then bring about is, however, something which takes place immediately *before* the action.

An example of a basic action could be the raising of (one of) my arm(s). Suppose one could "watch," one way or other, what happens in my brain and that one has been able to identify the neural event, or set of events, N, which must occur, we think, if my arm is to rise.[43] I say to somebody: "I can bring about the event N in my brain. Look." Then I raise my arm and my interlocutor observes what happens in my brain. He sees N happen. But if he also observes what I do, he will find that this takes place a fraction of a second after N. Strictly speaking: what he will observe is that the result of my action, *i.e.* my arm going up, materializes a little later than N occurs.

This is causation operating from the present towards the past. It must, I think, be accepted as such. By performing basic actions we bring about earlier events in our neural system. It would not be correct to try to restore the parallelism of causation and time here by saying that it was my *decision* to raise my arm which brought about N and that the decision is anterior to the happening of N. For I might have decided or intended to raise my arm and not carried out the decision (intention), in which case N might not have occurred at all. Only by putting my decision into effect, *i.e.* by actually raising my arm, do I do something which necessitates the occurrence of N. It is not what I decide or intend that matters to the occurrence of N, but the event, whether intentional or not, of my arm going up. And this event is such that I can see to it that it happens, *viz.* by *raising* my arm, but not just by *deciding* (intending) to raise it.

A crucial step in the argument which was designed to show that the direction of causation and time can be opposed was the assumption that we can identify some neural event as the necessary, or sufficient, condition of the result of a certain basic action. Let the end-state of this neural event be p and the result of the action q. We then have the nomic statement saying that p is a condition of a certain sort of q. How has this been established?

A neurophysiologist, let us assume, has studied the human brain and advanced a hypothesis: (the coming to be of) p is a necessary condition of (the coming to be of) q. In order to test it, he would have to make experiments. These would, roughly speaking, consist in preventing p from coming into existence and then noticing that q does not materialize either. If he had made the hypothesis that p is a sufficient condition of q, he would test it by producing p—say by stimulating a certain center in the brain—and noticing that q comes about, *e.g.* that a person's *arm rises* (that the person also maybe *raises his arm* would not be relevant to the physiologist's observation).

When a person raises his arm he sets in motion what I have called a "closed system." The initial state of this system is q, *e.g.* the arm in the upright position. To the system also belongs, we assume, another state p which, although temporally prior to q, is yet "causally posterior" to q, in the sense that by doing (so that) q we bring about (so that) p. In relation to this system q is a sufficient condition of p.

When the neurophysiologist interferes with the brain, he too sets in motion a closed system. The initial state of this system is p (or $\sim p$ as the case may be). There is another state in the system, q (or $\sim q$). The initial state is here both causally and temporally prior. By doing (so that) p (or $\sim p$) the experimenter brings about q (or $\sim q$).

We conclude ("inductively") from the observation of the succession of states *and* the fact, if it is a fact, that persons *can* raise their arms that the first chain of temporally related states (from q to p) is a closed system. That we can raise our arm presupposes that normally, from our daily life, we are familiar with situations when our arm is hanging down and will, we think, remain in this position, unless "we ourselves" raise it. We know, moreover, that normally when we decide, intend, or want to raise our arm now, the arm will rise, unless we cancel our decision or change our intention. Sometimes, of course, surprises occur. A man finds that he cannot in the current situation raise his arm, that he is disabled or prevented.

Similarly, we conclude from observations of regular succession and the fact, if it is a fact, that the experimenter *can* produce or suppress certain brain events that the second chain of states (from p to q or from $\sim p$ to $\sim q$) forms a closed system. That he can do this presupposes that he is familiar with situations in which he feels reasonably sure that a certain brain-state $\sim p$ (or p) will continue "under his eyes" unless *he*, the physiologist, changes it. And he also knows from experience that when he changes it, then with a fair amount of regularity, even though exceptions may occur, he will witness q (or $\sim q$). If the person subject to the experiment kept on raising his arm "at will" all the time, thus bringing about (in direction "backwards") shifts in p, this would "destroy" the situation for the experimenter so that he would not be able to claim confidently that *he can* produce or destroy p. But, conversely, if the experimenter constantly interfered with the brain so that the subject could no longer be confident that situations when his arm is hanging will continue unless *he himself* interferes, then he could no longer claim that *he can* raise his arm.

Any claim that there is a closed system with initial state p or a closed system with initial state q can only be substantiated provided there is some agent, outside these systems, who can operate them, put them in motion, by initiating their initial states in situations when he feels sure that they would not originate if it were not for his intervention. The same holds for every claim that a given system is closed.

When the agent sets the system in motion by raising his arm, the initial state q is produced from some anterior state. Of this state, as we have said before, the agent is confident that it will not change from being $\sim q$ to being q, *unless he changes it.* How is this state $\sim q$ related to the state p, which also precedes q? There are three possibilities to be considered.

The neural state p may obtain simultaneously with the state $\sim q$ which is the initial state of the action of raising one's arm. The "total state of the world" then includes both p and $\sim q$, although the agent either is not aware of p at all, or is aware of it, but ignorant of the fact that p is a sufficient condition of q. (If he were aware of p and thought it sufficient to produce q, he would of course *not* think that the state containing the state p will not change to q, unless he changes it.)

The neural state may, however, also come into existence after the initial and before the end-state of the action. The state which the agent changes to q is then not a state *immediately* preceding q, but a state separated from it by some distance in time. This indeed is how the situation is normally constituted. The initial state of an action (which results in a change and) of which we feel confident that it would not change unless we change it, is seldom strictly *the* immediately preceding state to the end-state of the action. Even a relatively simple action "takes some time" to perform. Between those states which in the "macro-description" of the world appear as the initial state and the end-state of an action we usually can, in a more finely graded description, insert intermediate state-descriptions.

The third possibility, finally, is that p is before the initial state of the action, but has not made noticeable to the agent its operation as a cause of q. If this were known to an outside observer, he would not say that p was brought about by the agent through retroactive causation. But he need not dispute that the agent raised his arm.

It is of some interest to note that "retroactive causation," if admitted at all, has, in any case, a *very short reach*. It never stretches in time beyond the obtaining of the state which the agent himself considers as the initial state of his action, the state which he, in acting, transforms into the result of his action.[44]

Any (generic) state which is the initial state of some closed system can be a subsequent state in some other closed system. There is no logical objection to this. To claim that this actually is the case with the initial state of a given system is to conceive of a possible agent who could bring about this state consequent upon producing the initial state of the more comprehensive system. Such a claim could be substantiated or upheld only if we know of an actual agent with this ability.

In the "race" between causation and agency, the latter will always win. It is a contradiction in terms to think that agency could be completely caught in the nets of causality. But all sorts of disabilities and incapacitations may befall an agent, due to the operations of causation.

Inasmuch as it is an empirical fact that a man *can do* various things when he decides, intends, wants to do them, he is, as an agent, *free*. To say that causation presupposes freedom would be misleading. It would suggest that the way in which laws of nature operate were somehow dependent upon men. This is not the case. But to say that the concept of causation presupposes the concept of freedom seems to me to be right, in the sense that it is only through the idea of doing things that we come to grasp the ideas of cause and effect.

The idea that causation can be a "threat" to freedom contains a fair amount of empirical truth, *viz.* the truths to which disabilities and incapacitation testify. But metaphysically it is an illusion. The illusion has been nourished by our tendency to think, in the spirit of Hume one might say, that man in a state of pure passivity, merely by observing regular sequences, can register causal connections and chains of causally connected events which he then by extrapolation thinks pervade the universe from an infinitely remote past to an infinitely remote future. This outlook fails to notice that causal relations are *relative* to fragments of the world's history which have the character of what we have here called closed systems. The discovery of causal relations presents two aspects: an active *and* a passive one. The active component is the putting in motion of systems through producing their initial states. The passive component consists in observing what happens inside the systems—as far as possible without disturbing them. The scientific experiment, one of the most ingenious and consequential devices of the human mind, is a systematic combination of these two components.

III

Intentionality and Teleological Explanation

1. Causality is traditionally contrasted with teleology, and causal explanation with teleological explanation. Causal explanations normally point to the past. "This happened, *because* that had occurred" is their typical form in language. It is then assumed that a nomic connection exists between the cause-factor and the effect-factor. In the simplest case this connection is a relation of sufficient conditionship. The validity of the explanation depends upon the validity of the assumed nomic tie between cause and effect.

Teleological explanations point to the future. "This happened, *in order* that that should occur." Here too an assumption of a nomic tie is involved. In the typical case the assumed connection is a relation of necessary conditionship. But the way in which this assumption is involved in the explanation is more complex, so to say oblique, than in the case of causal explanations. The validity of what I propose to call a "genuine" teleological explanation does *not* depend on the validity of the assumed nomic relation involved in it. If, for example, I say that he ran in order to catch the train, I intimate that he thought it (under the circumstances) necessary, and maybe sufficient, to run, if he was going to reach the station before the departure of the train. His belief, however, may be mistaken —perhaps he would have missed the train no matter how fast he ran. But my explanation of his running may nevertheless be correct.

The schematic forms of explicative sentences which we quoted above cover a multitude of different cases. There is by no means a one-to-one correspondence between the two forms of words and the two main types of explanation. Explanations which are not teleological are often couched in teleological terminology. If, for example, I explain the acceleration of the breathing movements in the lungs when a man is engaged in heavy muscular activity, such as running or climbing a hill, by saying that they speed up in order that equilibrium in the chemical composition of the blood be preserved, the explanation is not of the kind here called "teleological." It can be translated into a complex statement concerning conditionship relations. Should future physiological and biochemical investigations show that this statement does not hold true, the explanation would have to be rejected as false or would at least have to be modified.

We have already termed (Ch. II, Sect. 6) *quasi-teleological* such explanations as may be couched in teleological terminology, but nevertheless depend for their validity on the truth of nomic connections. Explanations of this kind more frequently answer questions as to *how* something is or became *possible* (*e.g.* for the blood to maintain relative stability in its chemical composition in spite of the drain of oxygen from it due to heavy exertion of the muscles), than questions as to *why* something happened *necessarily*. Functional explanations in biology and natural history are typically quasi-teleological as we have defined the term.

It is also a fact that by no means all explanations of the schematic form "This happened, because ——" are genuinely causal. "He screamed, because he felt pain" or "There was an uprising among the people, because the government was corrupt and oppressive" are explicative statements. Their *explanantia* refer to something that went before, not to anything which is ahead of the *explananda*. The second statement nevertheless has a teleological ring. The aim of the uprising was obviously to get rid of an evil from which the people had been suffering. The first statement could not, I think, be construed teleologically without distortion. But I would maintain that neither of them depends for its validity on the validity of a nomic connection. On this ground I shall call them *quasi-causal*. Such explanations figure prominently, it seems, in the behavioral and social sciences—are in fact characteristic of them. They help us to understand what something *is* (*e.g.* pain, and not horror) or for which reason (*e.g.* oppression) it happens.

A conceptual difference between causal and quasi-teleological explanations on the one hand and quasi-causal and teleological explanations on the other hand is thus that explanations of the former type depend for their validity upon the truth of nomic connections whereas explanations of the latter type do not—at least not in their overt form.[1]

One could object to calling quasi-teleological explanations "teleological" at all; and similarly one could object to calling quasi-causal explanations "causal." But one could also take another line and object to calling quasi-teleological and quasi-causal explanations "quasi."

Those who object to calling quasi-teleological explanations

"quasi" would probably wish to defend the view that these are the genuinely teleological explanations to which all other forms of teleology can be reduced (as science makes progress).[2] Those again who object to calling quasi-causal explanations "quasi" would probably wish to attack the experimentalist idea of causation which we discussed in the last chapter as too narrow. Against the former I should maintain that they are wrong;[3] against the latter again that I find the restricted terminology more useful for keeping clear distinctions which a more comprehensive terminology is apt to blur.[4]

Recently, the term *teleonomy* has been used by several authors to refer to adaptation in nature as the result of natural selection.[5] It would perhaps be feasible to give to the term an extended use referring to all forms of teleology which depend on nomic connections. "Teleonomy" would then be another name for what is here called "quasi-teleology."[6]

2. The *explanandum* of a teleological explanation is, in the typical cases, an item of *behavior*—or it is the product or result of behavior. "Behavior," however, is used in a very wide variety of senses. One talks of the behavior of a magnetic needle in the presence of an electric current. Such behavior is, of course, not explained teleologically. But it is noteworthy that reactions of inanimate objects are often described in "actionistic" language.

Behavior which has a genuine teleological explanation might be called *action-like*. Action, one could say, normally presents two aspects: an "inner" and an "outer."[7] The first is the intentionality of the action, the intention or will "behind" its outer manifestations. The second again may be divided into two parts or phases. I shall call them the *immediate* and the *remote* outer aspects of an action. The immediate outer aspect is muscular activity—*e.g.* a turning of the hand or raising of an arm. The remote outer aspect is some event for which this muscular activity is causally responsible—*e.g.* the turning of a handle or the opening of a window, or better: the fact that a certain handle turns or window opens. The remote aspect need not be a *change;* it can also consist in the fact that a change does *not* take place, as for example when I prevent a vase from toppling over by seizing it with my hand. The remote aspect can also be missing, as for example when I simply raise my arm. The immediate aspect, finally, need not be *movement.* It can also consist in the tension of muscles, as is typically the case in action which is "preventive" as distinct from action which is "productive" (or "destructive").

It should be observed that not everything which is ordinarily called an act (or an activity) has an outer as well as an inner aspect. Acts (activities) which lack an outer aspect are often called *mental.* The term "behavior" seems quite inappropriate for mental acts and activities. Also the term "action" is not normally used for them.

It should further be noted that not everything called action (or activity) has an inner as well as an outer aspect. Action (activity) void of intentionality is often called *reflex action.* Such action is also said to be the *reaction* or *response* of a (living) body to a *stimulus.*[8]

Only behavior which is action-like and has what we have called an inner *and* an outer aspect will concern us here.

Many actions have the character of a *performance,* in which case there is normally a phase of the outer aspect of the action which is such that unless it materializes the action has, by definition, not been performed (completed). This phase of the outer aspect we shall call (in a somewhat technical sense) the *result* of the action (cf. Ch. II, Sect. 8). The result is thus a phase (part) of the outer aspect which is *intrinsically* (conceptually, logically) connected with the action itself.

For example, the act of opening a window is a performance. Its result is the event (change) which consists of the window opening (changes from being shut to being open). Had the window not opened it would be logically wrong to describe what the agent did as an act of window-opening. It could still have been an attempt (effort, trial) to open the window.

The phase or phases of the outer aspect of an action which is not intrinsically connected with the action as its result I shall call either causal antecedents or effects of the result of the action, depending upon the nature of the causal relation of this phase to the result. The effects will also, in conformity with a familiar terminology, be called consequences (of the action). The consequences of an action are thus effects of its result.[9] (Cf. Ch. II, Sect. 8.)

For example, certain movements of my body are causal antecedents of the result of an act of window-opening. A drop in the indoor temperature may be a consequence (effect) of the same act.

The phase of the outer aspect (if it has many phases) which is regarded as the result of the action can usually be shifted (within the aspect). This shift answers to subsuming the action under different *descriptions*.[10]

For example, let the three phases of the outer aspect of a certain act of window-opening be the pressing of a button, the opening of the window, and a drop in temperature in a certain room. We can now describe what was done in the following three ways: the agent pressed the button and, as a consequence, the window opened and the room was cooled; or, the agent opened the window by pressing a button (causal antecedent) and as a consequence the room was cooled; or, the agent cooled the room by opening the window which he did by (first) pressing a button.

What constitutes the unity of the outer aspect of an action is not, be it observed, the causal tie linking its various phases. The unity is constituted by the subsumption of the phases under the same *intention*. What makes the anterior and posterior phases part of the outer aspect of the same action is that they can all be said to be *intentionally* done by the agent on that occasion. To use a phrase which has become current since the appearance of Anscombe's book, the behavior of the agent in our example is *intentional under the descriptions* "he opened the window," "he pressed the button," and "he cooled the room."

When the outer aspect of an action consists of several causally related phases, it is normally correct to single out *one* of them as the *object* of the agent's intention. It is the thing which the agent *intends to do*. This is the result of his action. The phases anterior to it are causal requirements and those posterior to it consequences of the action.

One must distinguish between intentional acting and intention to do a certain thing. Everything which we intend to do and also actually do we do intentionally. But it cannot be said that we intend to do everything we do intentionally. Nor does it seem indisputable that, whenever we do something intentionally, there is also something we intend to do, an object of intention. The movements which my hand performs when I am brushing my teeth are *intentional*; when I set myself to the activity I *intend to* brush my teeth—*not* to perform those movements. But the movements, for example, which my hand often make when I am talking seem not to be connected with an object of intention. Can we say they are intentional? The answer, I think, will have to depend on further particulars about the case—*e.g.*, whether the agent is aware of the movements, or not. But if the movements are intentional without being relatable to an object of intention, then there is no teleological explanation for them either. To explain behavior teleologically, one could say, is to pin-point in it an object of intention.

The question arises of how consequences of my action which are intentional are related to consequences which are foreseen. Consider again the example of the tripartite action of button-pressing, window-opening, and room-cooling. Assume that it is a further consequence of this action that a person in the room begins to shiver, and that the agent can foresee this. His intention, however, was not to make that other man shiver. It was, say, to let cool air into the room. Shall we say now that he *made* that other person shiver but that his acting was not intentional under that description? I doubt whether there are clear criteria for deciding. One could not say that he *unintentionally* made the person shiver, since he knew this was going to happen and he was acting intentionally. But neither does it sound correct to say, without qualification, that he intentionally made him shiver. The qualifications to be made here seem, moreover, to be of a *moral* nature. If the agent can be blamed for what he foresaw without intending to bring it about, then the foreseen consequence is something which he did intentionally and for which we hold him responsible.

Action has a "passive" counterpart which is usually called *forbearance*. Forbearance can be distinguished from mere passivity, notacting, by being intentional passivity. By forbearing one does not strictly produce things or prevent things from happening, but by forbearing one can *let* things change or *leave* them unchanged. These changes and not-changes are the outer aspect of forbearance. Again one can distinguish between an immediate and a remote outer aspect. The immediate outer aspect of forbearance is, normally, a state of muscular rest or, exceptionally, muscular activity which one "lets go on" although one could restrain the movements.

Is forbearance "behavior"? If one classifies forbearance as a mood ("passive") of action, there can be no objection to calling it a mood of behavior either. It is more important to note that forbearance may require *explanation* just as much as action, and that teleology or goal-directedness can be a feature of forbearance just as well as of action.

The distinction of forms of action and forbearance and the working out of an "algebra" or "logic" of action on the basis of these distinctions will not occupy us here.[11] Nor shall I take up for special discussion problems connected with (the explanation of) forbearance as distinct from action, or of productive as distinct from preventive action. But it is good to be aware of the dangers of onesidedness which may arise if the discussion is centered, in the traditional manner, only on action which is productive of changes. Preventive action and forbearance may have problems of their own worthy of attention.

3. The distinction which I have made between an outer and an inner aspect of action can, and should, be understood in an unproblematic sense. It does not prejudge the difficult question of the nature of the "inner." There is, for example, no claim that it is a mental act or process or a state of mind or an "experience." We shall also try to bypass this problem as much as possible. But it will inevitably lurk in the background as soon as we raise the further question of how the two aspects of action are *related*.

Explanation and Understanding

We have already made use of the common metaphor that the intention or will is something "behind" the outer behavioral manifestations of action. With this metaphor is coupled an idea which has played a very great role in philosophic thinking at least since the time of Descartes. This is the view of the will as a *cause* of behavior (bodily movements, muscular activity). If this view were true, then teleological explanations of behavior would be "translatable" into causal explanations. The goal "pulling from the future" could be replaced by the will (to reach the goal) "pushing towards the future." An extreme version of this view identifies the will itself with some states or processes in the body (brain), and is thus a form of materialism.

Consider an action, *e.g.* the ringing of a doorbell. Its result is that the bell rings. Can the intention or will to ring the bell cause this result? Obviously, it cannot do this directly. One cannot make the bell ring simply by willing. There must be intermediate links between the will and the result of the action—for example the raising of an arm and pressing of a button. If the will is a cause at all, it must be the *immediate* cause of the first temporal link (phase) in this series of successive events in the world and only a *remote* cause of the result of the action. The first link is the same as that which we have earlier (Sect. 2) called the immediate outer aspect of the action, and which consists in some form of muscular activity (or tension). We are thus imagining a causal chain in which the first cause-factor is the will, the first effect-factor the immediate outer aspect of the action, and the ultimate effect the result of the action.[12] (The chain may continue from the result to consequences of the action.) Is this imagination logically flawless (possible)?

Under one interpretation of the phrase it can be indisputably true to say that the (my) will was the cause of my action. This is if I mean simply that I rang the bell *intentionally* and not, say, by mistake. But this is trivial, and we are not thinking of this case when we raise the question of whether the will to ring the bell can be a (remote) cause of the bell's ringing.

As said at the beginning of Chapter II, philosophers, particularly since Hume, have been accustomed to distinguish between cause and effect on the one hand and ground and consequence on the other. The point of this distinction is to emphasize that a distinguishing feature of the causal relation is that cause and effect are *logically independent* of one another.

A causal relation which satisfies this requirement of logical independence between its terms I shall call *humean*. Using this name for it involves no commitment to the rest of Hume's views about the nature of causation, thus also no commitment to the regularity view.[13]

The problem before us is now: Can the intention or will be a *humean cause* of behavior, *i.e.* of the immediate outer aspect of an action?

Contemporary philosophers are sharply divided on this problem. Some regard it as (logically) possible and often true that the will works as a genuine, *i.e.* humean, cause of behavior. Others deny this. The latter then usually give as a reason for their opinion that the will is not logically independent of the behavior whose cause it is alleged to be. They maintain, in other words, that the connection between will and behavior is a logical and therefore not in the humean sense a causal relation.[14]

I think myself that those who advocate what has become known as the Logical Connection Argument are substantially right. But I am not sure whether anybody has as yet succeeded in presenting the argument quite convincingly. Some versions of it are not only unconvincing but manifestly defective.[15]

Several writers see the essence of the argument in the fact

that the intention or the will to do a certain thing cannot be *defined* without making reference to its object, *i.e.* its intended or willed result, and therewith also to the outer aspect of the action.[16] The will to ring the bell *differs* specifically from other acts of the will through its object, *viz.* the ringing of the bell. This observation is correct and pertinent. It implies that acts of the will differ interestingly from other things which may figure as (humean) causes and which *can* be defined without reference to their supposed effects. Thus, for example, the spark of fire which drops into the powder-barrel and causes an explosion can be unambiguously characterized and distinguished from other things in nature through its "intrinsic" properties, without any reference to the explosion which it may, or may not, bring about depending upon the circumstances. But it does not follow, from this difference between acts of will and a great number of so-called mental acts on the one hand and other things which may enter into causal relations on the other, that the will could not, nevertheless, be a (humean) cause of behavior. The logical dependence of the specific *character* of the will on the nature of its object is fully compatible with the logical independence of the *occurrence* of an act of will of this character from the realization of the object.[17]

A good way of tackling the logical connection argument is in terms of *verification*. Let it be asked how, in a given case, one ascertains (verifies) whether an agent has a certain intention, "wills" a certain thing—and also how one finds out whether his behavior is of a kind which his intention or will is supposed to cause. Should it turn out that one *cannot* answer the one question without also answering the other, then the intention or will cannot be a (humean) cause of his behavior. The facts which one tries to establish would not be logically independent of one another.[18] I shall try to show that an investigation of the problem of verification must lead to this result.

Throughout this section I have been speaking about "intention or will." The implication is not that I regard the two as being the same. But there was no need to distinguish between the two in the above sketchy presentation of the idea that the inner aspect of action could be a humean cause of the outer aspect.

In the sequel I shall be discussing only *intentions*. One reason why I shall not speak about acts of the will (or about willing) is that this largely is an artificial terminology invented for philosophic purposes, and is difficult to relate to the way we actually speak and think about actions.

For the sake of convenience I shall call those who think that the intention can be a humean cause of behavior *causalists*, and those who regard the connection between intention and behavior as being of a conceptual or logical nature *intentionalists*.[19]

Besides intentions and acts of the will there are a number of other mental concepts which are relevant to the question of causes of actions. These are decisions, desires, motives, reasons, wants, and still others. I shall not discuss them specifically here. But these other forces that prompt agents to act must also be fitted into a full picture of how the inner and outer aspects of an action are related. With regard to them, the picture as given here is incomplete. The reader should be warned against overhasty interpretations of my position. I argue against a "causal theory of action." But I am not denying that, *e.g.*, desires or wants could have a causal influence on behavior. Nor am I disputing the obvious role which dispositions, habits, inclinations, and other regularities and uniformities of behavior play to the explanation and understanding of action.[20]

4. Let us look at the following schema:

(PI) A intends to bring about p.

A considers that he cannot bring about p unless he does a.

Therefore A sets himself to do a.

A schema of this kind is sometimes called a *practical inference* (or syllogism). I shall use this name for it here, without pretending that it is historically adequate, and consciously ignoring the fact that there are many different schemas which may be grouped under the same heading.[21]

There are alternative forms of what I should regard as essentially the same schema as (PI) above. Instead of "intends" one can say "is aiming" or "pursues as an end" or, sometimes, "wants" in the first premise. Instead of "considers" one could say "thinks" or "believes" or, sometimes, "knows" in the second premise. Instead of "sets himself to do" one could say "embarks on doing" or "proceeds to doing" or, sometimes, simply "does" in the conclusion. *Setting* oneself to do something I thus understand in a way which implies that behavior has been initiated. I do not mean to suggest that all the alternatives mentioned are synonyms, but only that substituting one for another would not essentially alter the nature of the problems which we are here raising and the solutions which we are going to suggest.[22]

The schema of the practical inference is that of a teleological explanation "turned upside down." The starting point of a teleological explanation (of action) is that someone sets himself to do something or, more commonly, that someone does something. We ask "Why?" The answer often is simply: "In order to bring about *p*." It is then taken for granted that the agent considers the behavior which we are trying to explain causally relevant to the bringing about of *p and* that the bringing about of *p* is what he is aiming at or intending with his behavior. Maybe the agent is mistaken in thinking the action causally related to the end in view. His being mistaken, however, does not invalidate the suggested explanation. What the agent *thinks* is the only relevant question here.

Is an inference according to the above schema logically conclusive?

The question of validity of a practical inference is related to the two views of the relation of the "inner" and the "outer" aspect of action which I called causalist and intentionalist. If one regards practical inferences, when properly formulated, as logically binding, one takes an intentionalist position. If again one accepts the causalist view, one would say of practical inferences that the truth of their premises ensures the truth of their conclusions, but that this is a "causal" and not a "logical" entailment.

Thus the causalist does not maintain that the intention alone will bring about a certain thing, will move the agent to behavior of a certain kind. A further factor is required to make the causal mechanism operative: an opinion, belief, or insight that reaching the object of intention requires a specific kind of behavior. The alleged cause is thus of a rather complex and peculiar nature, which in itself may arouse doubts as to whether a cognitive-volitative complex of the kind in question can possibly function as a humean cause of anything at all. But let us not prejudge the answer.

If the relation between intention and cognition on the one hand and behavior on the other hand is causal, there is a general law (nonlogical nomic connection) involved. The premises of the argument instantiate the antecedent, the conclusion instantiates the consequent of this law. The law *and* the instantiated singular propositions logically entail the conclusion. Thus, in what is here called the causalist view, the practical inference (and therewith the teleological explanation) is only a disguised form of a nomological-deductive explanation in accordance with the covering law model.

5. Before tackling the question of the validity, logical or causal, of practical inferences we must settle a number of preliminary points concerning the form and content of the type of reasoning which our schema (PI) exemplifies. The first question concerns its purported relation to teleological explanations. Assume that A intends to bring about *p* and considers the doing of *a sufficient* to this end. Does it follow that he will set himself to do *a?* Surely not in any sense of "follow" which could claim to make the inference conclusive.

Assume that A sets himself to do *a*, or that he does *a*. Would we have given a formally satisfactory teleological explanation of A's behavior if we said that A intended to bring about *p* and considered the doing of *a* sufficient for this end? The question is perplexing. If we give it an unqualified affirmative answer, we admit that a teleological explanation of action is not just the "converse" of a practical inference of the type (PI), but is a much wider category. It does indeed seem feasible to give an affirmative answer, but it must be subject to certain qualifications.

If doing *a* is the *only* thing A considers sufficient for the attainment of his end, there is no problem. For then the doing of *a* is also, in his opinion, necessary. But assume there is more than one thing, say *a* and *b*, the doing of either of which A considers sufficient means to his end. Then he has a *choice*.

Intentionality and Teleological Explanation

Unless he chooses to do something which is sufficient to bring about *p*, he will not be able to achieve his end. In other words, it is *necessary* for him to do *one thing or other* which he thinks *sufficient* for the purpose of bringing about *p*.

If the practical inference is constructed in a way which makes it binding, the conclusion must be that A sets himself to do *a or b*. As an item of behavior on some given occasion, doing *a or b* will normally consist in the doing of *a*, but not *b*, *or* in the doing of *b*, but not *a*. The search for a teleological explanation legitimately allows the further question of why A chose to do *a*, and not *b*. There may be some further teleological explanation for his choice, *e.g.* that he considered *a* the cheapest, or the quickest, or the easiest way of bringing about *p*, and that he intended (wanted) to bring about *p* with as little cost, or as quickly, or as easily as possible. And to this explanation would correspond a practical inference ending with the conclusion that A sets himself to do *a*. But whether this additional teleological explanation can actually be given, and the corresponding inference actually be constructed, is a matter of contingent fact. There need not exist a reason for every choice. Choice, though necessarily intentional, may nevertheless be entirely fortuitous.

Thus, when we consider what the teleological explanation really succeeds in explaining, and what it leaves out, the "converse" relationship between practical inferences and teleological explanations is seen to hold true.

One could, however, also make the above observations a ground for relaxing the schema of the practical inference and broadening the notion of a teleological explanation of action. To say that A did *a* because he thought this would take him to his end of action *p* could be regarded as a fully satisfactory answer to the question why A did *a*. But it cannot be turned into a conclusive argument, unless supplemented by further

99

data about A's intentions and cognitions. In *this* respect the explanation is still "incomplete." One can proceed still further with the relaxation of the schema. Perhaps A thought the doing of *a* neither necessary nor sufficient for his ends, but considered that doing *a* may nevertheless in some way *favor* their attainment or increase the chances (probability) that he will reach them. Here too we can explain why he did A, without in the first place having a conclusive argument. And again one can try to complete the explanation by looking for supplementary premises. One way of supplying them would be to point to the *risks* which the agent runs of failing of his aims if he neglects certain measures. We can then regard avoiding the risks as a (secondary) aim of the agent. In this way, by giving a new twist to its first premise, we sometimes "restore" the argument to conclusiveness.

A second question of a preparatory character which we must discuss is the following:

Assume A considers the doing of *a* necessary for the bringing about of *p*, but also thinks or knows that he cannot do *a*. Would it still follow that he sets himself to do *a*?

One could answer that a man who thinks he cannot do a certain thing cannot, offhand, set himself to do it either. If he is not certain, he can try to do it.[23] If he feels sure he cannot do it, he will perhaps take some steps to learn to do it.

But one can also doubt whether a man who thinks he cannot do *a*, can even *intend* to bring about anything, say *p*, for which he considers the doing of *a* necessary. He may wish or strongly hope that *p* shall *come* about, e.g. because some other agent brings it about. He may want to learn how to bring about *p*—which entails wanting to learn to do *a*. He can be so strongly resolved to bring about *p* that the following practical inference becomes valid:

> A intends to bring about *p*.
> A considers that he cannot bring about *p*, unless he (first) learns (how) to do *a*.
> Therefore A sets himself to learn to do *a*.

The upshot is that, if the inference in the original form (PI) is to be valid, it must be assumed that the agent thinks he can do the things which are required for the fulfillment of what he intends to do.

Assume that A intends to bring about *p* and considers the doing of *a* necessary, *but not sufficient,* to this end. Does it then follow too that he will set himself to do *a?*

Two cases must here be distinguished. The first is, when A has an opinion of what would, in addition to doing *a*, be sufficient to bring about *p*, and also thinks that he can see to it that these additional requirements are fulfilled, *e.g.* by doing the required things himself. The second case is when A either does not know which the sufficient conditions for the bringing about of *p* are, or thinks that he knows them but also that he cannot satisfy them.

In the first case the answer to the question posed could be affirmative. In the second case the answer must be negative. A will not—unless for some different reason, not forming part of the argument—set himself to do *a*. For he now thinks or knows that doing *a* is no good for the end he has in mind. But this case also raises a problem:

Is the fact that A does not think he knows how to bring about *p* logically compatible with the assumption that he intends to bring about *p?* In other words, is the case we are imagining logically consistent? I think the answer is negative, independently of whether one takes an intentionalist or causalist stand on the question of the validity of practical inferences.

The nature of the case which we are considering becomes clearer, if instead of speaking about intending to do we (first) speak about wanting to do. Consider this example. I want to shoot down the wild goose flying there. I have a rifle in my hand. If I am to hit the bird I must aim at it with the rifle. But assume I have no cartridges left and thus cannot now load my gun, which is also necessary if I am to shoot the bird. Perhaps I nevertheless aim at the flying bird. This would then be only a "symbolic gesture" and not meant seriously as a step in the complex action of shooting the bird in the flight.

But can I, under the circumstances we have described, be said even to "want" to shoot the goose? I can certainly say, *e.g.*, "I wanted to shoot it, but found I had no cartridges left" or "I wish I could shoot it, but alas I have no more shots." I can also say, "I want to shoot that bird—I'll first get some more ammunition and then I'll pursue the bird; I know where it will be hiding." For "wanted" in the first sentence I can also without change of meaning put "intended," and for "want" in the last sentence "intend." Whether I can say, without talking nonsense, that I want to shoot the goose *now*, knowing that I cannot do this (now), seems to depend upon how we interpret the meaning of "want." If "I want to" means "I should like to," saying this is all right. If it means "I intend to," then the use of "want"—when combined with the "now"—appears logically inappropriate. I can intend to do—and therefore also "want" *in the sense of* "intend"—only such things as I think I can do, consider myself able to do. This is of course "legislating" about intention. I do not claim that the use of the word always carries with it this presupposition. But the cases when the word is thus used are important and it is with them alone that we are here concerned. It is therefore legitimate to separate these cases from other ones.

According to the view I am taking here, the first premise of the practical inference contains, in a concealed form, that the agent thinks he knows [24] how to bring about the object of his intention. This entails that he also thinks he knows how to perform the actions which he considers necessary and at least one action which he considers sufficient to this end. Thus the intention includes a cognitive element. The volitional and the cognitive aspects cannot be so separated that the former is completely included in the first premise and the latter completely in the second premise. The first premise necessarily exhibits both aspects. This does not make the second premise superfluous. From the fact that A intends to bring about p it does not, of course, follow that he specifically considers the doing of a necessary for this. His opinion of what the "situation requires" of him may be very strange indeed, may be completely erroneous or even superstitious. That he intends to bring about p only entails that he has *some* opinion of what is required of him, but not that he has any specific opinion. If it is part and parcel of this opinion that he has to do a in order to achieve his aim, but that doing a alone is not enough, then it is also part and parcel of this opinion that he has some idea of what *else* he has to do and that he thinks he can do the required residue as well, in addition to a.

6. In our original formulation of the inference schema (PI) no attention is paid to *time*. We have implicitly argued on the supposition that A (now) intends to bring about p now, (now) considers the doing by him of a now necessary to this end, and therefore now sets himself to do a.

Often, however, the object of intention is in the future. This is indeed normally the case when we say, without specifying the time, that we intend to do something. One can argue that this is so, even when we say we intend to do something *now*. For the "now" is then the time immediately ahead of us.

When the object of intention is in the future, it may nevertheless be the case that the circumstances require me to do something *now* in order to achieve the end. But what the circumstances require me to do can also often be deferred, at least for some time. Therefore the fact that I now intend to bring about something in the future need not, in conjunction with my views of what I have to do in order to achieve my end, terminate in any action at all on my part now.

I intend to travel from Helsinki to Copenhagen over the weekend. I know that, unless I book my passage in advance, I shall not be able to travel. But I can defer the booking another two or three days, need not do it now.

Would the following be a correct way of properly taking into account time in the formulation of a practical inference?

A (now) intends to bring about *p* at time *t*.

A (now) considers that, unless he does *a* no later than at time *t'*, he will not be able to bring about *p* at time *t*.

Therefore, no later than at time *t'*, A sets himself to do *a*.

But this inference schema obviously can*not* be binding—neither logically nor causally. Between now and times *t'* and *t* all sorts of things may happen. A may change his plans (intentions), or he may forget them. A may also change his view of what he has to do in order to achieve his aim.

In order to take into account these contingencies in our formulation of the inference schema, we must change the first two occurrences of "now" to "from now on," meaning by this the time between the present moment and t'. The schema then goes:

> From now on A intends to bring about p at time t.
>
> From now on A considers that, unless he does a no later than at time t', he cannot bring about p at time t.
>
> Therefore, no later than at time t', A sets himself to do a.[25]

These changes, however, are not enough. The statement that A sets himself to do something at time t' makes objective reference to time. But A may not know that time t' is there, when in fact it is; or he may think it is there, when in fact it is not. The most that can be claimed in the conclusion of the practical inference is that A sets himself to do a no later than when he *thinks*, rightly or wrongly, that time t' has come. The practical inference then becomes:

> From now on A intends to bring about p at time t.
>
> From now on A considers that, unless he does a no later than at time t', he cannot bring about p at time t.
>
> Therefore, no later than when he thinks time t' has arrived, A sets himself to do a.

But perhaps the moment when A thinks the time is due never comes. He *forgets about the time*. Then he forgets to (set himself to) do a as well. But it does not follow that he has given up his intention, or even that he can truthfully be said to have *forgotten his intention*.[26] The situation we are now envisaging is compatible with the truth of the counterfactual which says that, had A been asked, at any time between now and what he thinks is time t', whether he is going to do a no later than at that time, his answer would have been "Yes."

This would suggest that he had not forgotten his intention. (To have an intention from a certain time on does not entail that one is all the time "thinking about it.")

In order to take this last contingency into account, we must add to the conclusion a clause "unless he forgets about the time."

But even when time has been duly taken into account there is one respect in which the inference schema remains incomplete, and therefore also obviously inconclusive. The agent may be *prevented* from carrying his intention into effect. He breaks a leg, or is put in prison, or has a stroke and is paralyzed, or even dies. The preventive factor is here understood to be some event in the ("outer") world, the happening of which makes it ("physically") impossible for the agent to do the required thing at the required time. Whether or not the agent is, in this sense, prevented from doing something is intersubjectively verifiable.

The preventive factor can either intervene between the "formation" of the intention and cognitive attitude and the execution of the required action, or it can occur at the very moment when the action is going to take place. The first case is certainly the more common of the two. When it occurs it will normally affect the agent's plans by changing them. The agent will perhaps give up his original intention when he realizes that he cannot carry it into effect. Or he will modify his intention so as to make it conform to his reduced abilities. Perhaps he reconsiders what the situation requires him to do and comes to the conclusion that, after all, it is not (as) necessary for him (as he thought) to do *a*—he can also do *b* from which he has not been prevented. If the one or the other of these things is what happens, then the original practical inference so to speak "dissolves" and the question of testing *its* binding force never becomes acute.

There remains the case when the preventive intervention occurs at the very moment when the agent sets himself to do *a*. (We can here include the possibility that the intervention occurred earlier but remained unnoticed by the agent.) Then there is no time for changing one's intention or for reconsidering the requirements of the situation. The practical inference does not "dissolve," but has to be stated subject to this contingency. We can do this by adding yet another clause to the conclusion. It reads "unless he is prevented."

The following may be regarded as the final formulation of the inference schema, the binding force of which we are here investigating:

> From now on A intends to bring about *p* at time *t*.
>
> From now on A considers that, unless he does *a* no later than at time *t'*, he cannot bring about *p* at time *t*.
>
> Therefore, no later than when he thinks time *t'* has arrived, A sets himself to do *a*, unless he forgets about the time or is prevented.

7. The matter of dispute is whether the *tie* between premises and conclusion of a practical inference is empirical (causal) or conceptual (logical). But the premises and the conclusion are themselves contingent, *i.e.* empirically and not logically true or false, propositions. It must therefore be possible [27] to verify and to falsify—or at least confirm and disconfirm—them on the basis of empirical observations and tests.

We now turn to this problem of verification. I shall try to argue that a solution of it also leads to an answer to the question of the "tie" and thus of the validity of the inference.

We first consider the conclusion. How does one verify (establish) that an agent sets himself to do something, unless he is prevented or forgets about the time?

Explanation and Understanding

When something has actually been done, it may be relatively easy to establish that the result of the action, which is an event in the world, has materialized. We see a body go through certain movements and have good reason to believe that these movements cause, say, the opening of a window.

But in order to verify that A did *a* it is not enough to verify that the result of the action came about and to verify or otherwise make plausible that it was caused to come about by some muscular activity displayed by A. We must also establish that what took place was intentional on A's part, and not something that he brought about only accidentally, by mistake, or even against his will. We must show that A's behavior, the movement which we see his body go through, is intentional *under the description* "doing *a*."

If we can verify that A (intentionally) did *a*, we need not normally verify that he also *set* himself to do *a*. The second, one could say, is entailed logically by the first. But in a great many cases, verifying that A set himself to do *a*, *i.e.* verifying the conclusion of the practical syllogism, cannot be accomplished by verifying that A did *a*. For A may have set himself to do *a* and tried but failed or for some other reason left the feat unaccomplished. How shall we in such cases verify the conclusion of the practical inference? We have to show that A —*i.e.* A's behavior—was "aiming" at this performance, without hitting the target. But wherein does this aiming consist? It cannot consist solely in the movements A performs, even if they are exactly like the movements which normally initiate successful performances of *a*. For we should still have to show that they were intentional. And they need not, after all, be like movements typical of successful performances of *a*. Yet it may be true that A in those movements was aiming at the doing of *a*.

108

Intentionality and Teleological Explanation

It may in practice be easier to establish that A set himself to do *a* when in fact he did *a* than when he failed to accomplish it. But in neither case will the verification of the external aspect of behavior and/or its causal effects suffice for the purpose. In both cases we shall also have to establish the intentional character of the behavior or of the accomplishment, that it is "aiming" at a certain achievement, *independently* of whether it accomplishes it or not.

But to establish that a certain item of behavior aims at a certain achievement, independently of how it happens to be causally connected with the thing sought for, is to establish the presence in the agent of a certain intention and (maybe) cognitive attitude concerning means to ends. And this means that the burden of verification is shifted from the verification of the conclusion to that of the premises of a practical inference.

That an agent is prevented from doing a certain thing on the occasion under consideration, shall here mean that he is "*physically*" prevented from exercising an ability which, in the generic sense, he possesses.[28] (Cf. above, p. 106.) "Psychological" prevention, even when it assumes the form of a strong threat of physical violence, shall not count, because then the agent's abstention from an action is *intentional* forbearance. The border between the two types of case may not always be clear, however. Sometimes our reaction to danger or to a threat has the character of a reflex or panic reaction which makes it doubtful whether behavior is intentional or not. In the normal case, however, it is a relatively easy and unproblematic procedure to ascertain whether an agent is or is not physically prevented from exercising an ability.

Assume now that we have established that A *is*, on the occasion under consideration, prevented from exercising his ability to do *a*. How could we then show that he would have set himself to do *a*, had he *not* been prevented? The *only* way to do this, it seems, is to show the presence in him of an intention to do *a*, or to do something for the achievement of which he considers the doing of *a* required. Here too, the burden of verification shifts from the conclusion back to the premises of a practical inference.

The case when the agent forgets about the time is relevant only when it can be assumed that he has not *also* forgotten or changed his intentions. (For if the latter is the case, the statement under discussion can no longer be supposed to be the conclusion of a practical argument.) Therefore to establish a case of forgetfulness of this kind is, *ipso facto*, to establish the truth of the premises of a practical inference. And to establish that A, who was not prevented, would have set himself to do *a* had he *not* forgotten about the time can only happen by showing that *a* either was what A intended to do or was something he considered it necessary to do for the attainment of a remoter object of his intention.

8.   How does one establish that an agent, from a certain time on, intends to bring about a certain thing and considers the doing of a certain other thing necessary for attaining the object of his intention?

There is a facet of the verification problem which we shall touch upon only lightly. It concerns the time factor and possible changes in intentions and cognitive attitudes. Granted we have established that A *now* has a certain intention and cognitive attitude. How shall we be sure that he retains it *from now on* to a certain future moment? Must we go on verifying it all the time? And how is a *change* in intention and/or cognitive attitude established?

Intentionality and Teleological Explanation

Having an intention and a cognitive attitude need not lead to action immediately. But "negatively" they will have an impact on our behavior from the time of their (joint) formation to the time of execution. This impact consists in that throughout this interval the agent does *not* intentionally do or undertake anything which he thinks (knows or believes) will make the fulfillment of his intention impossible. If I have an intention to go and see my aunt tomorrow afternoon I do not tomorrow morning take a plane to Peking. If I did, one would have to say either that I have changed my mind (intention) or that I do not understand the requirements of the situation or that I am being carried away to Peking against my will. It is from the observation of some such behavior that we verify a change of mind. But the observation itself is a verification of the type we are now interested in, *viz.* the establishing of a present intention and/or epistemic attitude. To verify that an intention is changed or retained presupposes verification of intentions—and intentional behavior—in the present. This is why we need not here discuss more thoroughly the complications concerning the time factor.

There are several indirect ways of establishing that an agent has a certain intention and thinks the doing of a certain act required for its realization. He belongs, for example, to a certain cultural community, he has a set education and a normal background of experiences. On the basis of these facts about him we may take it for granted that he can bring about p and knows (or believes) that to this end he has to do a. He also possesses certain traits of character and temperament which dispose him to react in a characteristic way in recurrent situations. This knowledge about him may make it very plausible for us to think that he now acts with the intention of producing p by doing a. Sometimes we even say we *know* his intentions and cognitions. Perhaps he has fallen into the river and cannot get out and cries as loud as he can for help. Surely he then wants to get out of his predicament and thinks that unless he cries and is heard, he will not be helped, and unless he is helped he cannot be saved.

A "verification" of this type is obviously only hypothetical and provisional, not irrevocable and final. It is based on analogies and assumptions which are normally reliable, but which in the individual case may turn out to be erroneous. Perhaps the man in the water is perfectly safe and only simulates distress. The reliability of the analogies, moreover, is known to us from individual cases in the past which had the intentionalist features which we conjecture in the new instances on the basis of dispositions, features of character, habits, and the like. It would clearly be circular to try to make such generalizations the criteria of truth for individual statements concerning the presence of intentions and cognitive attitudes in agents.[29]

Are there then not more direct ways of finding out what a person intends and what he considers necessary to carry his intentions into effect? There is a method which we often resort to and which we normally regard as the one which of all external methods gives most direct access to the facts we want to ascertain. We ask the man why he is shouting. Let us assume that he answers in a language which we understand. His answer—spoken or written—is behavior too, verbal behavior. Let his answer be, say, "I am shouting for help in order to be saved from drowning"—perhaps a somewhat unlikely grammatical form of a statement in the predicament under consideration. Why does he give this answer? To answer this question is to *explain* his verbal behavior. The explanation could have the following schematic form:

A cries "help" in order to be rescued from drowning.

Intentionality and Teleological Explanation

A thinks that he will not be saved unless he does not
(truthfully) reply to the question why he is shouting.

Therefore, A says that he is shouting in order to be
rescued.

This is a practical inference. It raises the very same questions
as those which we are now trying to answer. Maybe A is lying.
If he is only simulating distress in shouting "help," he is also
likely to reply to the question why he does this by saying,
"I am shouting in order to be rescued." But then the above
explanation, that he says this in order to be rescued, would be
wrong.

So, if his words "I am shouting for help in order to be
rescued" verifies what he intends [30] and why he behaves as he
does (cries "help"), this is only because we take their truth-
fulness for granted. Be it observed, moreover, that the difficulty
of verification concerns not only the premises, but in an equal
measure the conclusion of the practical syllogism whereby we
explain the agent's verbal behavior. How do we establish that
A *says that* he is shouting in order to be rescued? What we
record are the sounds he produces. We can record that he says
"I am shouting in order to be rescued." But this is not yet
recording that he says he shouts in order to be rescued. For
how do we know that this is what he *meant* by his words?
When we take their meaning for granted and use this to support the truth of the premises of the original practical inference,
viz. the one terminating in the cry "help," we assume we have
already verified the conclusion of another practical syllogism,
viz. the one terminating in his saying something in reply to a
question.

Verbal behavior does not in principle afford more direct
access to the inner states than any other (intentional) behavior. When we realize this, it becomes tempting to say that

113

the only direct method of verification is the intending and acting agent's own awareness of his inner states. "Only I can *know* what I intend and what I think is needed for the realization of the object of my intention."

I am in front of the door and intend to ring the bell *right now*. How do I know that this is what I intend? The fact is that my pressing of the button—or whatever else it is that I now *do*—aims at making the bell ring. But in what way can this fact be said to be *known* to me? Must I reflect on the meaning of my movements whenever I act intentionally?

My knowledge of my own intentions can be based on reflective knowledge of myself, on observing and putting an interpretation on my reactions. In such cases knowledge of myself is just as "external" and "indirect" as that of another observer, and may be even less reliable than his knowledge of me. (It is by no means certain that I am myself the best judge of my own intentions, or of my cognitive attitudes, for that matter.) My immediate knowledge of my own intentions is not based on reflection about myself (my inner states), but *is* the intentionality of my behavior, its association with an intention to achieve something. It is therefore of no use for verifying the premises of a practical inference which say what my intentions and cognitive attitudes are, since it *is* itself the very thing which has to be established (verified), *viz.* the aiming inherent in my behavior.

Intentional behavior, one could say, resembles the use of language.[31] It is a gesture whereby I mean something. Just as the use and the understanding of language presuppose a language community, the understanding of action presupposes a community of institutions and practices and technological equipment into which one has been introduced by learning and training. One could perhaps call it a life-community.[32] We cannot understand or teleologically explain behavior which is completely alien to us.

Am I saying then that my intention (right now) to ring the bell and my thinking the pressing of the button necessary for this end is *the same* as the fact that I now press the button? To this should be answered: It is not the same as the sequence of bodily movements and events in the external world which terminates in my finger's pressing against the button and the button's sinking into the hole. But it is this sequence *meant* by me (or *understood* by others) as an act of ringing the bell.

To say that the intentionality is *in* the behavior is at once suggestive of something important and easily misleading. The truth in that formulation is that intentionality is not anything "behind" or "outside" the behavior. It is not a mental act or characteristic experience accompanying it. The misleading thing about the formulation is that it suggests a "location" of the intention, a confinement of it to a definite item of behavior, as though one could discover the intentionality from a study of the movements. One could say—but this too might be misleading—that the behavior's intentionality is its *place* in a story about the agent. Behavior gets its intentional character from being *seen* by the agent himself or by an outside observer in a wider perspective, from being *set* in a context of aims and cognitions. This is what happens when we construe a practical inference to match it, as premises match a given conclusion.

The result of our inquiry into the verification problem is thus as follows:

The verification of the conclusion of a practical argument presupposes that we can verify a correlated set of premises which entail logically that the behavior observed to have occurred is intentional under the description given to it in the conclusion. Then we can no longer affirm these premises and deny the conclusion, *i.e.* deny the correctness of the description given of the observed behavior. But the set of verified premises need not, of course, be the same as the premises of the practical argument under discussion.

The verification of the premises of a practical argument again presupposes that we can single out some recorded item of behavior as being intentional under the description accorded to it either by those premises themselves ("immediate" verification) or by some other set of premises which entail those of the argument under discussion ("external" verification).

In this mutual dependence of the verification of premises and the verification of conclusions in practical syllogisms consists, as I see it, the truth of the Logical Connection Argument.

It is a characteristic of these verification procedures that they presuppose the *existence* of some factual behavior, upon which an intentionalist "interpretation" is then put. Assume that no such behavior is there. What does this assumption amount to?

We have the premises of a practical argument: an agent intends to bring about something and considers the doing of something else necessary for this end. It is time for him to act. He thinks so himself. Perhaps he was resolved to shoot the tyrant. He stands in front of the beast, aiming at him with his loaded revolver. But nothing happens. Must we say that he is "paralyzed"? He is subjected to medical examination and nothing is found which would indicate that he was physically prevented from carrying his intention into effect. Must we say that he gave up his intention or that he revised the requirements of the situation? He refuses to admit either alternative. Must we say that he is lying? These questions aim at constructing a case in which to say that he was prevented, or forgot about the time, or gave up his intention, or reassessed the requirements of the situation would have no other foundation than the mere fact that he did not set himself to action in accordance with the premises. This is an extreme case, to be sure. But I do not see that it could not occur. In this case the only thing which would make us insist upon saying one or the other of the above things is that we turn the validity of the practical syllogism into a standard for interpreting the situation. This may be reasonable. But there is no logical compulsion here. We could just as well say: if this sort of case can be imagined, it shows that the conclusion of a practical inference does not follow with logical necessity from the premises. To insist that it does would be dogmatism.

It is a characteristic of the case which we were imagining that the agent should do literally *nothing*. This does not mean that the agent forbears to act. For since forbearance is intentional nonacting, intentionally abstaining from carrying the intention into effect is a change of intention. This would be a case when the syllogism "dissolves" and the question of its validity does not arise.

Thus, despite the truth of the Logical Connection Argument, the premises of a practical inference do *not* with logical necessity entail behavior. They do not entail the "existence" of a conclusion to match them. The syllogism when leading up to action is "practical" and not a piece of logical demonstration.[33] It is only when action is already there and a practical argument is constructed to explain or justify it that we have a logically conclusive argument. The necessity of the practical inference schema is, one could say, a necessity conceived *ex post actu*.

I have tried to show how the premises and the conclusion of a practical inference are *connected*. I have done this by means of considerations pertaining to their verification. A problem which we have not considered here is which of alternative sets of premises should be accepted for a given conclusion. This is the problem of testing the correctness (truth) of the "material," as distinct from "formal," validity of a proposed teleological explanation of action. *It* will not be discussed in the present work.

9. Granted that the premises of a practical argument do not describe a humean cause of the behavior described in the conclusion, the question of whether the same item of behavior could not also be explained causally still remains open. There are two opposed positions on this issue: the Compatibility Thesis, which answers the question positively, and the Incompatibility Thesis, which answers it negatively.[34] I shall try to show that both positions contain something which is true and something which is not true, and that therefore, properly interpreted, they are not opposed.

In order to make a confrontation of the two positions at all possible, we must first investigate whether for *the same explanandum* both a teleological and a causal explanation could be meaningfully proposed.

What *is* the *explanandum* of a causal explanation of behavior? An item of behavior, to be sure. But this is not an unambiguous characterization. It leaves open the question of whether it is behavior intentionalistically understood as being an action or otherwise aiming at an achievement, or whether it is behavior as a "purely natural" event, *i.e.* in the last resort muscular activity.

It may be convenient to describe the *explanandum* of a causal explanation of behavior in intentionalistic ("actionistic") language. A physiological experimenter stimulates the neural system of a human being in a certain way and this being accordingly "performs certain movements," *e.g.* lifts his arm. But the intentionalistic description of the movements as activity or action is irrelevant to their causal explanation as an effect of the stimulation, and may even be rightly considered not strictly "scientific." What is explained is why *parts of his body move*, under the causal influence of stimulations of his nervous system, and not why *he moves parts of his body*. (The latter he would do under the teleological influence of his intentions and epistemic attitudes.) We can, *e.g.*, photograph those movements, arrange the pictures in a frame of coordinates, and describe them as locomotion in this frame.

The question of what is the *explanandum* of a teleological explanation is more complex. One can pinpoint the difficulty here by raising the following question: Is it possible to *describe* the movements which are explained teleologically entirely in nonintentionalistic terms, *i.e.* describe them in such a way that behavior *under that description* is not intentional? Could one describe them, for example, as locomotion of some bodies in a frame of coordinates?

Consider once again the practical syllogism. Its conclusion is that an agent, unless he is prevented, sets himself to do a certain thing which he thinks required for the achievement of some end of his. When we want to explain behavior teleologically we start, so to speak, from the conclusion and work our way back to the premises. In normal cases we start from the fact that an action has been accomplished and can thus take it for granted that the agent also "set himself" to do it. We can, without evading essential difficulties, simplify things by restricting the discussion here to such normal cases only.

Let thus the item of behavior in need of a teleological explanation be—intentionalistically described—that A does a certain thing *a*, *e.g.* presses a button. We propose the following teleological explanation for it by constructing, in the past tense, premises of a practical inference to match this *explanandum* as conclusion:

A intended to make the bell ring.

A thought (knew) that unless he pressed the button,
   he could not make the bell ring.

Therefore A pressed the button.

This explanation can be "materially invalid" (false, incorrect) in the sense that the reason why A pressed the button was in fact different. But it is "formally valid" (correct) as an *ex post actu* construction of premises to match a given conclusion.

Now let us see whether one could replace the conclusion by a nonintentionalistic description of A's behavior and *retain the formal validity of the explanation* (inference). We try the following, the premises remaining as before:

Therefore A's finger pushed against the button.

This sentence might be true—but *it* could not be necessary under the premises. Buttons can be pressed in many different ways. It may not be necessary to use one's fingers for the purpose at all. A man, moreover, normally has ten fingers. Perhaps he pressed the button with his right hand thumb. Even if he had to use his fingers to press the button, it cannot follow logically from the premises, as we have stated them above, that he had to press it with some particular finger.

How then shall we formulate the conclusion in nonintentionalistic terms without vitiating the formal validity of the explanation? Consider:

Therefore A's body moved in a manner which caused
   pressure against the button.

This proposal would not be acceptable either. A is breathing and the stream of air from his mouth, generated through his breathing, exerts, let us assume, a weak pressure against the button. This behavior would not normally count as falling within the orbit of the teleological explanation at all. Why? Obviously, because we should not ordinarily interpret this as an act of pressing the button. But if, from the position of his body and the twist of his mouth and the way he breathed, we had come to think that he was blowing towards the button, then we might *a fortiori* have interpreted what he did as a strange way of button-pressing.

In the situation which we are imagining there occurs behavior, *viz.* movements in A's body. These movements can certainly be described in a way which is drained of all intentionality.[35] But if it be asked which of them are such that their execution follows logically from the premises of our practical inference above, the answer would have to be that they are those movements which we interpret as an act of pressing the button. The conclusion to match the premises thus is:

Therefore A's body moved in a manner which constitutes an act of pressing the button.

But this is only another, and more involved, way of saying that A pressed the button. We are back where we started.

The upshot of the argument is thus as follows: the formal validity of the practical inference requires that the item of behavior mentioned in its conclusion is described (understood, interpreted) as action, as the doing or trying to do something by the agent under consideration. In order to become *teleologically explicable*, one could also say, behavior must first be *intentionalistically understood*. The interpretation can be guided by an explanation which we have at hand for the case. For all we can think, we may say, the man in front of the door means to ring the bell and knows that he has to press the button. So the rather strange movements we see him go through obviously aim at pressing the button. Later we perhaps discover that his

Explanation and Understanding

arms are crippled and he has to use his feet for doing such things as button-pressing.

The end in the terms of which the action is explained can be more or less "remote" from the action itself. For example: A presses the button in order to make the bell ring. Thus by pressing the button he makes the bell ring. But A rings the bell (makes the bell ring) in order to be let in. Thus by ringing the bell he is let in and also: by pressing the button he is let in.

But what if the behavior has no further end at all but is, as we say, "an end in itself" or done "for its own sake"? Also in the example which we have been discussing, it is not necessary to assume any end behind the action itself. A just presses the button. He does not do this in order to make the bell ring. *Perhaps* he does it just in order to make the button sink into the hole. Then we could explain his action as follows:

A intends to make the button sink into the hole.

A thinks he cannot achieve this unless he presses the button.

Therefore A presses the button.

But this need by no means be a valid explanation (of the button-pressing). Perhaps the *only thing* A meant to do was to press the button. Perhaps he had never before in his life done that sort of thing. He has seen other people do it, but he does not know what for. The performance looks easy. He wants to try it himself. And so he presses the button.

For the case when the action itself is identical with the object of intention, and not a means to the attainment of this object, one cannot construct an explanation of the form of a practical inference. The second premise is missing. There is only the first premise and the conclusion (*explanandum*). The first premise is: A intended to press the button. The conclusion, depending upon the peculiarities of the case, is either: A set himself to press the button, or: A pressed the button, or: A would have set himself to press (or would have pressed) the button, had he not been prevented. Assume that it is the second. We can then form a "mutilated" inference:

A intended to press the button.

Therefore A pressed the button.

This sounds pretty trivial. Can it be the "explanation" of anything? It would not be quite correct to say that it is the explanation of an *action*. The action of pressing the button is not explained by saying that it was intentional, willed. For that it was this is already contained in calling it an action. If we want to *explain the action,* we must therefore be able to point to some more remote end or object of intention which is not *in* the action itself. But if we want to explain or, which would be a better form of expression here, to *understand the behavior* which has taken place in the situation under consideration, then it would *not* be trivial to say that A intended to press the button. That is, it would not be trivial to interpret that which happened as an act of pressing the button. Perhaps A's behavior in the situation was very strange. Let us assume that he pressed the button with his elbow. We should then perhaps be hesitant as to what he was really doing: did he press the button or did he perhaps do something else, *e.g.* scratch his elbow, from which it followed accidentally that the button was pressed? Such cases can be imagined.

"A pressed the button because he intended to press the button." This is not an explanation of why A pressed the button. But it can be a somewhat misleading way of saying that, in pressing the button, A had no ulterior object of intention than precisely that—to press the button.

"A behaved the way he did because he intended to press the button." This can be said to have a genuine explicative force, when it means that A's behavior was intentional pressing of the button or an attempt to press the button, and not only a movement of some part of his body which resulted in pressure against the button. When thus we "explain" A's behavior, we understand it as the outer aspect of an action by spotting an intention in it.

The mere understanding of behavior as action, *e.g.* button-pressing, without attributing to it a remoter purpose, *e.g.* making a bell ring, for the attainment of which the action is a means, is itself a way of explaining behavior. Perhaps it could be called a rudimentary form of a teleological explanation. It is the step whereby we move the description of behavior on to the teleological level, one could say. But it seems to me clearer to separate this step from explanation proper, and thus to distinguish between the *understanding of behavior* (as action) and the *teleological explanation of action* (*i.e.* of intentional-istically understood behavior).

We can now answer the questions which we raised earlier about the sameness or difference in the *explananda* of causal and teleological explanations. The *explanandum* of a teleological explanation is an action, that of a causal explanation an intentionalistically noninterpreted item of behavior, *i.e.* some bodily movement or state. Since the *explananda* are different, the question of compatibility does not arise at this level. But this does not yet solve the problem. For *the same* item of behavior which is the *explanandum* of a causal explanation may also be given an intentionalistic interpretation which turns it into the *explanandum* of a teleological explanation. So the question of compatibility remains in this form: Can the same item of behavior be both validly causally explained as movement and correctly understood as being an action? [36] This is the question we must discuss next.

10. Consider some relatively simple action such as the raising of my arm, the pressing of a button, or the opening of a door. The result of such an action is an event in the world: the rising of my arm, the sinking of the button into the hole, the door's opening. In the second and third case, moreover, this event is something which occurs "outside" my body.

In order that an action be performable, there must be an *opportunity* for its performance.[37] There is an opportunity for raising my arm only if it is not already in a risen position, for pressing a button into a hole only if it is not already there, and for opening a door only if it is shut. This much is clear and un-controversial. More problematic is the following question: If an agent "seizes" the opportunity and performs the action, must it then be true to say that, had he not performed the action on that occasion, the event which is the result of the action would not have happened? An affirmative answer would entail that there is, in a characteristic sense, a *counterfactual element* involved in every action. (Cf. above, Ch. II, Sect. 7.)

Assume the door is shut but opens "of itself" at the very moment when I am about to open it. I have already grasped the handle and begun to push and my arm is now following the movement of the opening door. Would it be right to say that I opened the door? The opportunity for me to do so vanished so to speak from under my hand.

The critical point is in the phrase "of itself." What does it mean? Obviously it does not mean here (as it sometimes does) that the event, the movement of the door, took place without any cause at all. It means rather that the cause, whatever it be, of the event was somehow operating independently of the behavior of the agent. For example, the door was pulled open from the other side, or the wind blew it open. These would be clear cases of independently operating causes. More complicated would be a case in which the opening of the door was due to a mechanism which was "released" through the agent's behavior. A beam of radiation, say, was broken as the agent stepped up to the door. The operation of the cause was then not independent of the agent's behavior (though independent of his seizing the handle, pushing, *etc.*). Shall we say that it was nevertheless independent of *the agent*, though not of his behavior? Two cases must now be distinguished.

Either the agent was aware of the mechanism and knew how it works, or he was not. In the first case it is right to say that he opened the door. He did this by walking through the beam, not by seizing the handle and pushing. (The last mentioned behavior was accidental to his act of opening the door, unless he thought something like, "Perhaps the mechanism is out of order; I had better do these other things, too, which will in any case open the door.") In the second case it is not right to say that he opened the door. The door opened for him, just when he was about to open it. The fact that *his behavior caused* the opening of the door does not entail that *he* opened the door, since the behavior which made the door open was not meant (intended) to have this effect. This is the sense in which we can say here that the door opened "of itself" and was not opened *by him*.

But if the agent, in our example with the beam, seized the handle and followed the opening door with his arm, then surely he *did* something. Indeed, he did at least seize the handle and push. This was intentional. In doing so, moreover, he aimed at opening the door. He set himself to do this last. But did he also accomplish the feat?

Could we not say here that he opened the door, since the causal efficacy of his bodily movements, we think, would have effected the opening of the door even if that other cause had not operated? The result of the action was simply causally *overdetermined.* But could we not also say that he did *not* open the door, since on that very occasion he was *prevented* from doing it through loss of opportunity? I think that we are, in fact, free to say either, and that the choice between the two ways of describing the case would depend upon further particulars about the situation. Perhaps we feel a little doubtful whether the pressure he applied with his arm was actually sufficient to have opened the door; then it was after all not *he* who did it. But if we are quite sure that what in fact he (undoubtedly) *did—viz.* his display of muscular activity—was sufficient to accomplish the opening of the door, then we should be more inclined, it seems, to ascribe an act of door-opening to him too, though the result of this act was overdetermined.

Generalizing, we can say that if the result of an action which an agent intends to accomplish by doing certain other things materializes "of itself," this phrase being understood as explained above, then what the agent *undoubtedly does* on the occasion in question "shrinks," or is "confined" to those things by the doing of which he meant to perform his action. Thus the (subsequent) discovery of a cause operating independently of the agent may lead to a *redescribing* of his action under, so to say, a "mutilated" aspect.

We sometimes make such "retractive" moves in our descriptions of action, but they are exceptions and not the rule. If such cases were much more common than they actually are they would probably modify our present views of how far human action "penetrates" the world in which we live. One could advance a hypothesis that in every case of, say, door-opening there has been and will be a hidden cause operating independently of the agent so that in fact no man ever opened a door. There would be no sure way of disproving this hypothesis, but there are also no good reasons for believing it.

There is, however, a limit to this process of redescription of actions. The limit is set by the basic actions. These, it will be remembered, are actions which are performed directly and not by doing something else of which their result is the causal effect.

Arm-raising need not be a basic action. I can conceive of various means, by the operating of which I can make my arm rise. But arm-raising can be, and normally is, a basic action.[38]

Is it true to say "I raised my arm" only provided it is also true to say that, had I not raised my arm, my arm would not have risen?

I have no intention to raise my arm, but somebody suddenly seizes it and raises it. The movements and the ensuing position are exactly those which could have resulted from my raising my arm. Now I could not say that I raised my arm, nor could I say that, had it not been for me, it would not have risen. I could, of course, say the latter and *mean* that had I not let him do it, but resisted, my arm would not have risen, or that had I not collaborated by lifting it a little this would not have happened. This may be true. But if "had it not been for me" means "had it not been for my raising my arm" it would be false.

What would decide whether I raised my arm or not on some occasion when there is no ostensible cause operating from outside my body? Assume my arm suddenly rises. Did I raise it? The answer could be: I had no intention whatsoever to raise my arm, but suddenly up it went. If this is the answer, then I did *not* raise my arm. Or the answer could be: I was just going to raise my arm, I had in fact decided to do this, when suddenly I noticed it rise. If this is the answer, then too I did not raise my arm. The opportunity was, as it were, lost for me. But the answer could also be: Surely I raised my arm—this was intentional. Then I also ought to be able to explain *how* it was intentional, *i.e.* fit it into a story about myself—for example by saying that I had decided to do it, or by saying that I was engaged in a discussion on the freedom of the will and wanted to prove to my opponent that I could raise my arm then "at will," or by saying that I raised my arm to reach a book from the shelf, thus explaining the action teleologically. If it were then pointed out to me that a certain event in my brain had just occurred which we think is a sufficient condition of my arm's rising, I need not withdraw my initial answer, but could just say: Well, I see, my arm would have risen in any case. This is not saying that the event had, as it were, two "causes": the neural event and me. It is saying that *the interpretation of behavior as action is compatible with the behavior having a humean cause.*

If a humean cause of my arm's rising operates, my arm will rise of "necessity," *i.e. natural* necessity. If I intend to take a book from the shelf and consider the raising of my arm (causally) necessary for this, then normally I raise my arm unless prevented. This is a statement of *logical* necessity. But between the events on the two levels, the level of natural and that of logical necessity, the relation is *contingent*. That a case of arm-rising is also a case of arm-raising is neither necessitated nor excluded by the operation of the cause, if there is one, which makes my arm go up.

It is nevertheless also true that, *on the whole*, I can say with confidence that my arm will remain in its present position (we shall assume it is not raised) *unless I raise it*. That I should have this confidence is, moreover, necessary if I am to say truthfully of myself that I *can* raise my arm. (See above, Ch. II,

Sect. 7.) But this confidence, and the fact that I can raise my arm, does not conflict with the possibility that, every time my arm goes up, there is a sufficient condition, causally responsible for this event, operating in my nervous system.

What is excluded, however, is that at one and the same time I raise my arm and *observe* the operation of the cause. For, observing the cause operate entails letting *it* lift my arm ("under my watching eyes"), and leaving it to the cause to do this is incompatible with lifting my arm myself. This is a logical ("grammatical") point. When I observe, I *let* things happen. When I act, I *make* them happen. It is a contradiction in terms both to let and to make the same thing happen on the same occasion. Therefore no man *can* observe the causes of the results of his own basic actions.

The events which are the results of basic actions thus happen, on the whole, only when we "vest" these events with intentionality, *i.e.* perform the basic actions. That this should be so is an empirical fact, but a fact which is fundamental to the *concept* of an action. The conceptual basis of action, one could therefore say, is partly our ignorance (unawareness) of the operation of causes and partly our confidence that certain changes will happen only when we happen to be acting.[39]

Suppose we agree that a certain generic neural event is a sufficient cause of the generic event of my arm's rising, but also wish to maintain that had this event not occurred on an individual occasion under consideration my arm would nevertheless have risen. What could be our grounds for maintaining this? One possible ground could be that we think the event has more than one humean sufficient cause and that some of these other causes operated, or would have operated, on the occasion in question. Perhaps we have empirical evidence for this.

Intentionality and Teleological Explanation

Whether or not there will be such evidence cannot be settled *a priori*. But if we have no *such* ground for our affirmation, could we then find any grounds for it? Could we not say that whether there was a humean cause or not, *I* would have raised my arm and so it would have risen? We should then also have to give some further reason, such as that we had decided to do this or were after something. And could we not be right? *Must* every event have a humean cause whenever it happens? [40] I think the most that can be maintained here is something on these lines: "for all we know" events such as arm-raising have, in each instance of their occurrence, humean causes, although we are not ordinarily ourselves aware of their operation. But this belief must be a belief founded on empirical evidence. We cannot prove it true *a priori*.

IV

Explanation in History
and the Social Sciences

1. A teleological explanation of action is normally preceded
by an act of intentionalist *understanding* of some behavioral
data.

One can distinguish "layers" or "orders" of such acts of understanding. For example: I see crowds of people in the street
moving in the same direction, shouting things in unison, some
waving flags, *etc*. What *is* it that is going on? I have already
understood the "elements" of what I see intentionalistically.
The people are "themselves" moving and not being swept away
by a wind or torrent. They are shouting—and this is to say
more than that sounds emanate from their throats. But the
"whole" which I observe is not yet clear to me. Is this a
demonstration? Or is it perhaps a folk festival or a religious procession that I am witnessing?

I do not think one could answer these questions by constructing teleological explanations for the (intentionalistically

understood) behavior of the individual members of the crowd. A demonstration has a purpose which can somehow be "extracted" from the purposes of individual men. But in what way it can be extracted is not easy to say. A folk festival or religious procession is only remotely, if at all, connected with purposes. Perhaps some people took part in the festival in order to amuse themselves. This would explain their presence on the occasion. But knowledge of their, and other participants', purpose in joining the crowd would not tell us that what is going on is a folk festival. (If we were told that their purpose was to join a folk festival, we should not be helped, unless we had independent criteria for judging whether something is, or is not, a folk festival.)

The answer to the question what is going on here is not a teleological explanation of the actions of individual men. It is a new, second-order act of understanding. From the fact that a man intends to press the button in front of him, we said, it does not follow that he performs certain specific bodily *movements* (or one of a number of specified alternative movements). It only follows that with the movements he performs he means to press the button. And similarly, from the fact that a crowd demonstrates, it does not follow logically that its members will perform certain specific individual actions (or one of a number of specified alternative actions). It only follows that the actions they perform are intended to be a demonstration or else their intention has been interfered with (e.g. the police have fired at the crowd and now the crowd is dispersing). The analogy between the case of individual and collective action could be worked out in great detail.

One can ascend in the hierarchy or orders of such interpretative acts of grasping a meaning. There have been demonstrations, riots, strikes, terrorism, *etc.* Is the situation to be labeled a "civil war" or a "revolution"? This is neither a question of classification according to given criteria, nor of arbitrarily deciding about the application of a term. It is a question of interpretation, of understanding the meaning of what is going on.

One might call this activity of interpretation *explicative*. Very much of what would normally be referred to as the "explanations" offered by historians and social scientists consists in such interpretations of the raw material of their research.

But it seems to me clearer to distinguish here between interpretation or understanding on the one hand and explanation on the other. The results of interpretation are answers to a question "What *is* this?" [1] Only when we ask *why* there was a demonstration, or which were the "causes" of the revolution, are we in a narrower and stricter sense trying to explain what there is, the facts.

The two activities, moreover, seem to be interconnected and to support each other in characteristic ways. This is another reason for separating them in a methodological inquiry. Explanation at one level often paves the way for a reinterpretation of the facts at a higher level. Again there is an analogy with individual action. An explanation in teleological terms of an act of pressing a button may result in our redescribing what the agent did as an act of sounding a bell or of calling people's attention or even of being let into a house. "By pressing the button he did *x*." We henceforth see what he did primarily as an act of *x*'ing. And similarly for collective action. Something which used to be thought of as a reformatory movement in religion may with a deepened insight into its causes come to appear as "essentially" a class struggle for land reform. With this reinterpretation of the facts a new impetus is given to explanation. From the study of the causes of religious dissent we may be led to an inquiry into the origin of social inequalities as a result, say, of changes in the methods of production in a society.

With every new act of interpretation the facts at hand are colligated under a new concept.[2] The facts, as it were, take on a "quality" which they did not possess before. This conceptual process is, I think, *related* to that which in hegelian and marxist philosophy is called the transmutation of "quantity into quality," [3] and also to various ideas which philosophers have entertained about "emergence" ("emergent qualities").

Before explanation can begin, its object—the *explanandum* —must be described. Any description may be said to tell us what something "is." If we call every act of grasping what a certain thing is "understanding," then understanding is a prerequisite of every explanation, whether causal or teleological. This is trivial. But understanding what something is in the sense of *is like* should not be confused with understanding what something is in the sense of *means* or *signifies*. The first is a characteristic preliminary of causal, the second of teleological explanation. It is therefore misleading to say that understanding *versus* explanation marks the difference between two types of scientific intelligibility. But one could say that the intentional or nonintentional character of their objects marks the difference between two types of understanding and of explanation.

2. Is there room for (genuine) causal explanation in history (and social science)? The answer is that there is certainly room for it. But its place is peculiar and in a characteristic sense subordinate to other types of explanation.[4]

It is convenient to consider separately the two main types of causal explanation which we distinguished earlier, *viz.* explanations in terms of sufficient conditions and explanations in terms of necessary conditions. The first answer questions of the

schematic form *Why necessary?* and the second questions of
the type *How possible?*

An archaeologist excavates the ruins of an ancient city. He
has come to think that the city must have suffered a catastrophe
some time around the year x and was virtually destroyed. What
was the cause of its destruction? Was it an earthquake, or was
it a flood, or was it enemy conquest? This is a problem for a
causal explanation of certain events in the physical world:
the falling down of bridges, the collapsing of walls, the toppling of statues, *etc.* The fact that one of the suggested *explanantia* (enemy action) presupposes an intentionalistic interpretation of some behavior does not affect the "causal purity" of
the explanation. For this interpretation is inessential to the
explicative force of the argument. To say that the city was
destroyed by men means that certain events, resulting from
the actions of men, brought about the destruction of the city.
These events were the causes, independently of whether or not
they were the results of action.

It is worth considering the relevance for historiography of an
explanation like the one we just mentioned. *That* the city dis-
appeared may be historically relevant in a variety of ways; *e.g.*
because of the way this fact affected cultural, economic, or
political developments in the neighboring cities or kingdoms.
These "effects" may be interesting to trace. Similarly, it may be
interesting to trace other recorded facts from that period back
to their "cause" in the destruction of the city. *Why* the city
perished, the actual cause of its destruction, would normally be
thought much less interesting to the historian. Whether the
cause was a flood or an earthquake may be completely irrelevant
to him. That the city was destroyed by men, and not by natural
forces, is not as such, *i.e.* as a *cause* of the collapsing of houses,
etc., interesting. But it may lead the historian to inquire into
the reasons ("causes" in the nonhumean sense) for this violent

aggression. The results of the inquiry might illuminate the role of the city and of its aggressors in the life of those times.

Generalizing and simplifying one could say something like this: causal explanations which look for sufficient conditions are not *directly* relevant to historical and social research.[5] (I am not counting as historiography the "natural history" of the universe, or of the earth, or of the development of the species.) But they may be indirectly relevant in two typical ways. One is when their *explananda* have interesting "effects" on subsequent human affairs. The other is when their *explanantia* have interesting "causes" in antecedent human actions and conditions. The role of the causal explanation proper is often to link the nonhumean causes of its *explanans* with the nonhumean effects of its *explanandum*. Thus, for example, if the destruction of the city was an act of envy or revenge on the part of a neighboring city and if the destruction in turn became an economic disaster for the entire region, we have established a link between *the rivalry of the two cities* and subsequent *changes in the economic life* of the region. *This* is the kind of connection the historiographer is interested in. The following schematic picture could be used to illustrate the case:

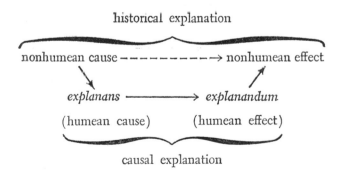

historical explanation

nonhumean cause – – – – – – – – – → nonhumean effect

explanans ——————→ *explanandum*

(humean cause)   (humean effect)

causal explanation

A somewhat different position is held in history and social study by causal explanations of the *How possible?* type.

Explanation and Understanding

An archaeologist excavates a city and is impressed by the colossal stones used in the city wall. How could the ancient inhabitants transport those blocks of stone and raise them to their proper position in the wall? The answer would make reference to some technological equipment or skill which those people are known or conjectured to have possessed. Thanks to this it was *causally possible* for them to achieve those feats. Similar causal statements would be involved, *e.g.* in an explanation in terms of natural conditions of how a nation could survive or defend itself successfully against a strong enemy. Such explanations are genuinely causal, since they depend for their validity on the existence of a nomic connection (and not only on a belief in this connection) between *explanantia* and *explananda*. The *explananda* are states or events in the world, *e.g.* that the stones came to be in the wall or that people continued to live in a certain region. The *explanantia* are other states or events which are causally necessary for the existence or coming into being of the first.

Again one can ask what relevance causal explanations of this kind have to historiography. In order for them to have any relevance at all, their *explananda*, it seems, must be *results* of action—individual or collective. When this condition is fulfilled, the relevance of the explanation lies in its giving an answer to the question how the *actions* were possible (not why they were undertaken). The following schema illustrates this case:

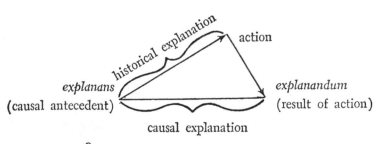

138

We may then proceed to explain how the actions, thus shown to have been possible, relate to other achievements of the same agents. But *this* is no longer explanation in terms of humean causation and nomic connections.

3. Prominent among the traditional tasks of historical explanation has been that of finding the "causes" of wars, revolutions, the rise and fall of empires, and great migratory movements. We shall here consider the following example, as good as any for our purposes:

Let the suggestion be that the cause of the outbreak of the First World War was the assassination of the Austrian archduke at Sarajevo in July 1914. We need not here take seriously the objection that this was only *one* cause among many and moreover not a very "deep" one. In the given constellation of circumstances the Sarajevo incident was nevertheless the "spark which made the powder-barrel explode." [6]

Here we have a given *explanandum*: the outbreak of the war, and a proposed *explanans*: the shots at Sarajevo. The critical historian's task would be to test the explanation for (factual) correctness. The philosopher's task is to investigate the conceptual nature of the mechanism connecting the *explanans* (the "cause") with the *explanandum* (the "effect"). Could this connection, this tie, for example be a covering (causal) law?

One thing seems clear which, superficially at least, speaks in favor of the possibility that the connection is genuinely causal. This is that *explanans* and *explanandum* obviously satisfy the requirement of being logically independent. Surely the killing of the archduke was a different event from the outbreak of the war. I shall not dispute this. But it may be mentioned in passing that the question of independence is not quite as simple as it may appear. The outbreak of a war is a complex event, composed of a great many "parts" of rather different character: political decisions, military orders, armed units starting to move, violent clashes resulting in bloodshed and destruction, *etc.* It is not self-evident that one can describe the event which we call the *outbreak* of the First World War without including the incident at Sarajevo in the description. But let us assume, at least for the sake of argument, that this can actually be done.

How then did the assassination cause the outbreak of the war? Surely it did not do this in literally the same way as a spark makes a barrel of gunpowder explode. The simile may after all be highly misleading and the mechanism at work in the two cases completely different. In both cases there are intermediate links between cause and effect which must be made clear before we understand the connection. In the case of the Sarajevo incident—but not in the explosion incident—these links are, typically, *motivations* for further actions.

Let us see—in rough outline—what actually took place after Sarajevo. In the first place, the assassination of the archduke caused the Austrian ultimatum to Serbia. The ultimatum gave Russia an excuse for mobilizing its army. This in turn fortified the Serbians in their attitude to the Austrian threat. When the Serbian government refused to comply with all the conditions of the ultimatum, the Austrian declaration of war on the Serbs followed. And so forth. But let us return to the first step, the ultimatum. Why did the Austrian cabinet issue it? Would it have issued a similar ultimatum to Denmark, if the archduke on a pleasure trip to Greenland had been killed by a mad eskimo? Hardly. The Sarajevo incident affected the aims and the interests of Austrian politics quite differently. One of the traditional pursuits of the Habsburgs had been to maintain and extend Austrian influence in the Balkans. This influence might have been seriously weakened unless those found guilty of the murder were punished, the conspiracy behind the assassination tracked down with all its possible ramifications abroad, and an assurance given that the interests behind the assassination would not be allowed to interfere with the current Austrian plans to organize an independent Croatian kingdom to counterbalance the influence of Russia in the Balkans. These considerations provided the raw material of motivations for the Austrian cabinet in making the "practical inferences" which terminated in the issuing of the ultimatum. Had the Austrian cabinet not issued it, then either its political aims would have been different from those which we attribute to it in our sketch of an explanation, *or* its assessment of the "requirements of the situation" would have been different. This we could then have concluded from its passivity. The conclusion would, moreover, have been of a logical kind. Between the ultimatum and its motivation background, as reconstructed by the historian, there is a conceptual connection, although the assassination and the ultimatum—and *a fortiori* the outbreak of the war— are logically independent events. The role of the murder in the nexus of successive events is that it changed the factual situation which the Austrian government had to assess with a view to drawing the appropriate practical conclusions for its actions. Thus, indirectly, the murder also changed the motivation background for the actions of the Austrian government. The (re)actions of the Austrians again affected in a similar manner the motivation background for the actions of the Russian government, and thus gradually, "by force of circumstances," the war became, as the saying goes, inevitable.

The example can be generalized. The explanation of events in history (*e.g.* the outbreak of a war) often consists simply in pointing out one or several earlier events (*e.g.* an assassination, a breach of treaty, a border incident) which we regard as its "contributory causes." If the antecedents are called *explanantia,* then *explananda* and *explanantia* in such historical explanations are indeed logically independent. What connects them, however, is not a set of general laws, but a set of singular statements which constitute the premises of practical inferences. The conclusion which emerges from the motivation background given in these premises is often not the *explanandum* itself, but some other, intermediate event or action—in our example the Austrian ultimatum—which enters into the motivation background of yet another practical inference with another intermediate conclusion—say Russia mobilizing her army—and so forth through a number of steps, until eventually we reach the *explanandum* itself.

To call the shots at Sarajevo a cause of the 1914–1918 war is a quite legitimate use of the term "cause"—only we must remember that we are not now speaking about humean causes and nomic connections. And to call the explanation "causal" is also quite in order so long as we do not assimilate it to explanations which fit the covering law model. To call the explanation "teleological" would certainly be a misnomer, although teleology essentially enters into the practical inferences which link the *explanans* to the *explanandum.* When, *faute de mieux,* I call it quasi-causal this does not imply any value judgment or imperfection of it as an explanation. I use the term because the explanation does not depend for its validity on the truth of general laws. (Cf. Ch. III, Sect. 1.)

We shall make a few more observations about the general structure of the explanation exemplified by the Sarajevo incident.

We have a sequence of independent events: the assassination, the ultimatum, ———, the outbreak of the war. The events are linked, we said, through practical syllogisms.[7] But *how?* The premises, as we sketched them, of the practical inference which led to the issuing of the ultimatum give us the motivation background for the action of the Austrian cabinet. Its first premise, it will be remembered, was about the aims and ends of Austrian politics. The second stated that a certain action, *viz.* the issuing of the ultimatum, was considered necessary lest the fulfillment of these aims be seriously endangered. A description of the assassination does not form part of either premise. To the first premise it need not be relevant at all. But to the second it is. The shots had created *a new situation*. In this new situation a certain action *became* necessary which—the aims and ends of action being the same—had not been necessary before. One could say that the event, *viz.* the assassination, "actuated" or "released" a practical inference which was there "latently." The conclusion of the actuated inference, *i.e.* the issuing of the ultimatum, created another situation, actuating a new practical inference (on the part of the Russian cabinet) which again created a new situation (the mobilization), actuating further practical inferences, the final "conclusion" of which was the outbreak of the war.

The following schematic picture could be used to illustrate this—a dotted arrow meaning that a fact affects the premises of a practical inference and an unbroken arrow that a new fact emerges as a conclusion from the premises:

quasi-causal historical explanation

practical
premises

explanans   *explanandum*

4. The aims and ends in the background of an explanation of the type we have studied are sometimes the rather subtle products of cultural, political, religious, *etc.* traditions. The origin and articulation of these aims can be another worthy object of historical explanation. But sometimes the motivation background is of a very "crude" and universally human character, so much so that it need not merit special consideration by the historian. Thus, for example, when the "causes" of a migratory movement of a tribe are said to be overpopulation or a famine or a flood. "They simply had to leave their homes." But could those people not have stayed on and let themselves be starved to death or drowned like rats? Of course they *could*, and perhaps some of them did. But on the whole people are anxious to save their lives from catastrophes and to look for a place where they can be fed or secure, if the conditions under which they live become intolerable. These are universal motives and need not be mentioned in the historian's explanations, which then immediately relate the *explananda* to antecedent changes in external circumstances, as the "effects" of given "causes."

There are certain main groups of changes in external circumstances which researchers of various schools have emphasized particularly strongly, or even perhaps wanted to regard as the sole or the most fundamental cause of events in history. One such group consists of changes in climate, the effects of erosion, and other events in the physical environment which necessitate adjustments in behavior and ways of life. A second group consists of changes in technology. They make it causally possible to accomplish things which before could not be done. Changes in the means of production are a subgroup of this.[8]

A reason for calling such changes "external" is that they make new actions either necessary under the changing causal impact of natural forces or possible thanks to the invention and mastery of new causal mechanisms. Such changes can be contrasted with changes in the "internal" circumstances of motivation (needs and wants) and cognitive attitudes of men. The question may then be raised as to how changes in circumstances of the one kind are related to changes in circumstances of the other kind, and which changes are "causes" and which "effects" relative to one another.

Probably one could not substantiate for any group of factors here an exclusive claim to be basic in the sense that changes in all the other groups can be derived from changes in it. This could hardly be done even for some more restricted type of claim such as that all changes in motivation can be traced back to changes in technology, let alone in the means of production. It may be true that the desire to do new things largely comes with a newly discovered possibility of doing them. But the advances in technology which make the doing of new things possible also have a motivation background. This background may have shifted in the course of history and the shifts conditioned, say, by changes in religious attitude rather than by other changes which are themselves of a technological character.[9] And technological changes may also be conditioned by external physical factors.[10]

Paradigmatic claims like those of, for example, historical materialism cannot be proved valid on *a priori* grounds. But they are not easily refuted on the basis of experience either.[11] The prime measure of their truth is their fertility for furthering our understanding of history or the social process. And this fertility may be considerable.[12]

5. The answer to the question why something was done is often that the agent was *made to do* it. Ways of making people do things constitute a distinct explanatory pattern, though one not unrelated to other patterns.

There is a variety of ways in which people are said to be

made to do things. One case is when an agent (or group of agents) is made to do things by some other agent (or group). Subcases of this general case may also be distinguished. Agents can make other agents do things by commanding (ordering) them to perform, or refrain from, actions; or by simply requesting certain things of people; or by threatening, intimidating, or blackmailing them; or by using physical violence (compulsion).

One characteristic use of physical violence is for *disabling* people, temporarily or permanently, from doing certain things, *e.g.* by imprisoning or mutilating them. This is, often enough, a purely causal mechanism, operated by the user of violence. What it does to the victim is essentially to destroy or suppress states which are causally necessary for the doing of various things. The causal mechanism at work in such cases sometimes has an oblique use for explaining why people did *not* do certain things which we take it for granted they would normally have done for some general motivational, usually teleological, considerations. Why did the prisoner not escape, although the door to his cell had been left open? The answer could be that he was chained to the wall. The causal explanation here is of the prisoner's *inability to do* a certain thing, and *not*, immediately, of his *not doing* it.

It is a noteworthy asymmetry that physical compulsion can make actions causally impossible, but not causally necessary. If a person grabs my arm and slaps another person in the face with it, *I* did not hit that other person's face and *a fortiori* cannot be said to have been compelled to do it either. The hitting was done solely by the person who used violence on me. When action, as distinct from forbearance, is necessitated by compulsion, compulsion is not "purely physical." If I hand over my purse to the robber at gun-point, I do so in order to save my life or from some other teleological motive. "I was compelled" now means "Had I not done so, then something would have happened which I did not at any cost want to happen." Had I wanted to be killed, I should not have been compelled to hand over my purse to the robber.

Is the mechanism causal when people do things in response to orders or requests? Such responses can be almost "mechanical." They sometimes bear an uncanny resemblance to reflex actions. The agent, who by his action calls forth a reaction in the subject, is not unlike the experimenter who through an act of interference with nature puts in motion a causal system. Not without reason can the activity of both be described as "manipulation."

In order to see more clearly the conceptual nature of the "making-people-do-things" mechanism it is helpful to compare the case where one agent makes another agent do something with another typical case where the mechanism is still operated from "outside" the agent but by the impersonal force of a norm or rule. People do things because the law of the state or of God requires it, or because the customs of the society or the codes of honor and good manners thus prescribe. We can group these various but related cases under the heading of *normative pressure.*

The way people respond to norms in the individual case need not be teleological at all. But the way in which norms come to exert a "pressure" on agents has clearly teleological characteristics.

To rules of conduct may be attached a *sanction, i.e.* a punitive reaction of some sort consequent upon a breach of a rule by somebody. In the case of legal norms, the nature and application of the punitive reaction is itself regulated by norms (laws of procedure, *etc.*). Deviation from the codes and customs of the society are apt to provoke the disapproval of a substantial part of the community, to be frowned upon. This is sanction too.

People sometimes conform to a norm in order not to be punished or reprimanded. What they do or refrain from doing has then a clear-cut teleological explanation.

Evasion of sanction is not the only teleological aspect of obedience to norms, however. The enacting of laws is often, or even usually, motivated by purposive considerations. Customs may originally have served purposes which later have been forgotten or become obsolete.

When the agents who are subject to normative pressure share the purposes for which the norms were made, they can be said to conform or obey in order that these purposes be fulfilled. The teleological mechanism, however, is not exactly similar to the schema of a practical inference which we studied in the previous chapter.

If a man obeys a law *because* he approves of the aim or purpose which the law is supposed to serve, he need not be convinced of the necessity of his personal contribution for securing the fulfillment of this purpose. But he must have some faith in the possibility of the purpose being fulfilled and in the necessity of a *collective* effort to secure this. One can approve of the aim for which a law or rule was made and at the same time be completely convinced of the unattainability of the aim. Action in accordance with the norm cannot then be explained as undertaken *in order to* secure the purpose of the norm. It may have been undertaken in order to set an example and encourage others. But then the agent must believe that the example is worth while, *i.e.* may ultimately lead to a situation in which the purpose of the norm will be secured by the co-operative efforts of the subjects.

Normative pressure is thus built up under the joint teleological influence of fear of sanction and anxiety to secure the ends for whose attainment the norms are considered instrumental. This does not mean that behavior conforming to norms has a teleological explanation in every single case. Neither fear of sanction nor zeal for the public good need be the reason why people conform.

Something closely analogous also holds true of the simpler cases where one agent makes another do things by commanding, requesting, *etc.* In the case of commands or orders one could speak of the *pressure of authority.* As children, we are taught and trained to obey and otherwise adequately to respond to commands and requests. We are taught this by means of teleological mechanisms for escaping punishment and seeking reward. At a later stage the teleology of the very action of "making do" often acquires motivational force for the subjects of such action. We come to think that the injunctions and prohibitions are there for the sake of our own "true good" or aim at securing our cooperation for ends which are ultimately also our own.

One could call the ends for the attainment of which commands or rules are instrumental *internal rewards* for obedience. Failure to attain those ends one could call *internal punishment* for disobedience. Rewards and punishments which attach to a norm but which do not consist in attaining or failing to attain the aim of the norm can be called *external.* The reason why external punishment holds a more basic position than external reward in the teleology of normative pressure can hardly be due to anything else than the fact that compliance with norms is also thought to be, in a majority of cases, internally rewarding to those who obey. There is thus a conceptual reason for this often observed asymmetry in the roles of reward and punishment.

It is thanks to its teleological background that the mechanism of making agents do things becomes operative. In this it differs from a causal mechanism. But the teleological background can be more or less remote from the individual case in which the mechanism operates. It can be so remote as to be completely missing from the individual case. This happens when the answer to the question of why an agent did such and such is that he did it *merely* because he had been commanded or *merely* because this is the custom, rule, practice, *etc.* of the society where he belongs. In the absence of *all* teleology behind the response in the individual case to stimulation through the mechanism, behavior often seems pointless, stupid, or irrational.

A making-do mechanism can also *lose* a part or the whole of its teleological background. This happens when the sanction ceases to be effective or reward ceases to be attractive. In these cases too, actions performed *merely* in response to stimulation through the mechanism acquire an air of irrationality.

It is against such forms of irrational behavior that moral and social critics often protest. Through their criticism they may pave the way for a more "meaningful" application of the various forms of pressure of authority and norms in a society.

Can response to the type of stimulation which we are now considering become so "mechanical" and void of a teleological motivation that it deteriorates into a form of conditioned reflex (re)action? *Can* the connection between stimulus and response here be a truly nomic (causal) connection? I do not see why this might not be the case. But such cases, I think, are rare. If they occur, the response would lose its character of being an action. For if it follows like a "reflex" upon the stimulation, the reacting subject can no longer confidently claim that, in situations when the stimulus is applied, the change which is supposed to occur would not happen, *unless he (as an agent, intentionally) makes it happen*. This confidence, as we have seen, is a logical prerequisite of action. If it is missing, the reaction is drained of intentionality. Then it is no longer *meant* as a response to the stimulation. It just *is* this.

6. It is important to distinguish between norms which regulate (enjoin, permit, or prohibit) conduct and rules which define various social practices and institutions. Both are called "norms" or "rules." A reason why they are easily confused is that they are at the same time characteristically different and intricately related.

Norms of the first kind tell us *that* certain things ought to or may be done. Norms of the second kind tell us *how* certain acts are performed. Often, but not in all cases, a norm of the second kind is needed in order to make compliance with a norm of the first kind possible. Norms of the second kind are therefore, in a characteristic sense, *secondary* in relation to the first. In order to keep the two types of norm or rule separate I shall here, *faute de mieux,* refer to them as primary and secondary norms (rules) respectively.[13]

In order for a marriage to become legally valid, the partners have to satisfy certain conditions (*e.g.* concerning age and perhaps mental and physical health) and go through certain ceremonies involving other parties who also have to fulfill certain conditions (*e.g.* be officials of some sort of the church or of the state). These conditions and ceremonies define the social action of getting married. Performance of this action has a number of "legal consequences." The married couple is allowed to establish a household, the partners have certain legal claims with regard to one another and responsibilities for their offspring, *etc.* These "consequences" are, normally, a set of norms of conduct, violation of which is likely to provoke sanctions on the part of the legal machinery of the society. The rules for getting married do not by themselves oblige anybody to anything; but the rule, if there is one, which prohibits unmarried people from establishing a household obliges them to abstain from doing this as long as they have not "performed the action" of getting married. People cannot be punished for not marrying (unless there is a law making marriage compulsory); but they can be punished, if unmarried, for doing things which only married people are allowed to do—or, if married, for neglecting things which are married persons' obligations.

Norms of this kind are not only extremely important in legal contexts. They pervade the whole of social life. The rule that one greets a lady or senior by doffing one's hat, or by making a bow, defines a practice. The rule of good manners which prescribes that a man should greet a lady or a senior, is different. It is a norm of conduct. A person who fails to comply with it may be excused on the ground that he is a stranger to the community and does not know how to greet, *i.e.* does not know the rules which define the practice (ceremony) of greeting. A person who can be supposed to know the rule but does not comply is subject to sanction, will be "frowned upon" by the society.

Secondary rules, as far as I can see, play no characteristic or important role in the *explanation* of behavior. This is so because they are not mechanisms for making people do things. But they are of fundamental importance to *understanding* behavior, and therefore to the descriptions which anthropologists and social scientists give of the communities which are the objects of their study.[14]

"Why did that man take off his hat and bow when he passed that lady in the street?" The answer could be: "He greeted her." But it could also be: "Because he wanted to pay her his respects." If the first, we are saying what the person was doing and thereby making his behavior intelligible to one who is not familiar with our conventions for greeting. (He is supposed to be familiar, though, with the notion of greeting people.) The second answer might be, or might hint at, a teleological explanation of the action. One could say that the first answer "really" matches a question "What?" and not the question "Why?"—but this would be pedantic. One could also say that the second answer "really" matches the question "Why did he greet the lady?" and not the question "Why did he take off his hat?" But that too would be pedantic.

7. What look like causal explanations in the sciences of man are usually explanations of the kind I have called quasi-causal. The question may be raised as to whether apparent teleological explanations in these fields are not sometimes explanations of the kind we called quasi-teleological.

Quasi-teleological explanation is primarily at home in biological contexts. "The breathing movements accelerate in order to compensate for the blood's loss of oxygen." We see a function in relation to a purpose. This is quasi-teleology. Is there anything analogous to it in history or social science? The question could also be put as follows: Do individual men and groups exhibit behavior which fulfills a purpose without being intended to do so? A related form of the same question is: Can men serve a "destiny" which is not definable in terms of their own intentional aims?

Consider the following case: The economic recovery of Poland under Casimir the Great was largely due to the fact that Jews who had been expelled from German territory were allowed and invited to settle in Poland. The expulsion of the Jews from Germany and their reception by the Polish king made possible the recovery of Poland. It would not be incorrect to say that the Jews *had to* leave Germany *in order for* Poland to flourish. Nor would this statement conflict with the truth that they *had to* leave Germany, *because* they were persecuted.

Generally speaking, the achievements, experiences or sufferings of one man or group of men sometimes *make possible* certain achievements, not contemplated before, of another man or generation or group. The earlier achievements or events then take on a new *significance* in the light of the later ones. They acquire as it were a purpose, unknown to those who were responsible for the achievements. This is *one* facet of the phenomenon that Hegel called the "List der Vernunft," the cunning of reason. In such cases we sometimes say that it was the "destiny" of those men to pave the way for a future which they themselves perhaps never contemplated. This is an innocuous use of "destiny" and of "purpose." But does it show that the explanations which we give of those earlier achievements in the light of the later ones are quasi-teleological?

The answer is plainly negative.

When we attribute significance to a past event on the ground that it made possible some later event, or even say that the first was needed in order for the second to come about, we are sometimes, but far from always, affirming a nomic connection of necessary conditionship between the events. The relation between some technical innovation and subsequent actions whose accomplishment this innovation made possible is (involves) a relation of nomic necessity. But the relation between the persecution of the Jews in medieval Germany and the boom of Poland under Casimir the Great, complex as it may be, involves no nomic (causal) connections. This holds true even if a historian could rightly claim that but for the events in Germany, Poland would not have flourished as it did. The one event is just as little a causally necessary condition of the second as the shots at Sarajevo were, under the circumstances, a causally sufficient condition of the 1914–1918 war. In both cases the link between the events is a motivational mechanism, whose working can be reconstructed as a series of practical inferences. The events to which a causal role is attributed create a new situation and thereby provide a factual basis for practical inferences which could not have been made before. But there is a characteristic difference between the two cases. It seems to be this: events in history "necessitate" other events when they make people reassess the "requirements of the situation" with a view to aims and intentions already existing. Events in history "make possible" other events when they reshape the intentions by providing agents with new opportunities for action. As long as capital and skilled labor are missing, plans for developing a country's economy remain futile wishes or are not even made. With the advent of those resources, implicit wishes mature into well-formed intentions and actions follow where impotence reigned before.

The process of reviewing the remote past in the light of the more recent past is a highly characteristic feature of the scholarly pursuit called historiography. It explains, why—for conceptual reasons—there can be no such thing as a complete or definitive account of the historical past. The reason is not merely that hitherto unknown facts may come to light. This is true but relatively trivial. The interesting reason is that the historian's efforts to understand and explain the more recent past leads him to attribute to the more ancient past a role or significance which it did not possess until more recent events had occurred. And since we do not, on the whole, know what the future will have in store we cannot now know the full scope of what is characteristic of the present and past either.[15]

A complete understanding of past history, one might say,

presupposes that there will be no future, that history has come to an end. There was a great philosopher who, in certain moments of exaltation, seems to have thought that he had "seen through" history completely. This philosopher was Hegel. At such moments he spoke of himself as being the end and consummation of world history.[16] But his words, I think, were meant to be taken with the grain of salt necessary to appreciate their truth.

The feature of historical research that the same past is constantly dug up anew is sometimes referred to as a process of revaluating the past. But this characterization is easily misleading. It makes the historian's judgment seem a matter of his tastes and preferences, of what *he* happens to consider important or "valuable." There is this element too in historiography, to be sure. But essentially the attribution of new significance to past events is not a subjective matter of "revaluation" but a matter of *explanation* with, in principle, objective tests of correctness. The statement, *e.g.*, that an earlier event x made possible a later event y may not be conclusively verifiable or refutable. But it is a statement grounded on *facts*, and not on what the historian *thinks* about them.

8. Purposefulness of the type which I have called quasi-teleology can often be accounted for causally with the aid of the idea of negative feedback. Why do the breathing movements accelerate when the body is engaged in heavy muscular activity? The answer that this happens in order to restore a disturbed equilibrium in the chemical composition of the blood announces the discovery of certain causal connections here. Muscular exertion drains the blood of oxygen and accelerated breathing restores it. But the question which this answers is not, strictly speaking, *why* breathing *must* accelerate but *how*

the blood *can* retain its chemical equilibrium. To think that the first question too has been answered by the announcement of those discoveries would be, I think, to accept an illegitimate "vitalist" idea of teleology in biological contexts. The final answer to the question of why breathing accelerates has not been given until we have announced the discovery of an additional causal connection which explains how the draining of oxygen from the blood accelerates the breathing movements. This connection is the feedback. With its discovery we have a "full" causal explanation of the case. We can now answer the question of why breathing accelerates, by reference to antecedent sufficient conditions, and not only, as in the quasi-teleological explanation, by reference to necessary conditions of subsequent events.

The discovery of the feedback, one could say, supplements a previous *How possible?* explanation with a new *Why necessary?* explanation. It thereby removes from the case the "air of teleology" which it had as long as the explanatory circuit was not complete.

Is there anything analogous to this in history and the life of societies? The question falls into two parts. Are there societal feedback processes? Are these processes instances of humean causation?

In feedback there is a concatenation of two systems. Let us call them the primary and the secondary systems. A certain amount of the primary system's causal efficiency is deflected into the secondary system so as to keep it "informed" of the operations of the first. This inflow of information makes the cause-factor of the secondary system operative. The effect is fed back into the primary system and "orders" a modification to take place in the operation of its cause-factor. This closes the chain of concatenated operations.

Calling the input into the secondary system "information" and its output, which is at the same time an input into the primary system, an "order" or "signal" is only partly a metaphor. The theory of the structure of the coded and decoded messages between the systems is in a literal sense information theory. The only metaphorical aspect is the allusion to the analogy between this causal exchange of messages and the intentional use which agents make of signs for linguistic communication.

Now think of a case where actions of agents can be said to steer a society in a certain direction through the decisions which they make effective, by building up "normative pressure" and perhaps by the occasional use of such means as physical compulsion or violence. Assume there is a part of the society which does not participate in the decision-making of the power group but which is informed about the results and enlightened enough to reflect about their consequences—both those which are intended by the decision-makers and the remoter ones which the decision-makers do not clearly foresee. This insight, more or less well articulated, may then call forth in that other group a desire to influence the power group so as to give its efficacy a new direction or otherwise temper it. In the absence of institutionalized channels for communicating new directives to the power group, the "feedbackers" will have to resort to forms of communicative action such as demonstrations, protests, strikes, sabotage, *etc.*, which are not regulated by existing rules of the social game and are sometimes even contrary to these rules.

The pattern of social action I am describing is familiar. Its analogy to the process called negative feedback is striking. But it should also be obvious from the schematic description given here, in combination with what has been said before about

158

"causes" and "effects" on the level of agents and intentional action, that the working of the feedback process is not humean causation under covering laws but motivational necessitation through practical inferences.

The deflection of information from the primary system is an influence on the cognitive attitudes of the agents belonging to the secondary system. It thus works on the second, or cognitive, premises of latent inferences. Unless an effort is made to adjust the working of the machinery of the primary system, a certain good cannot be attained or a certain bad averted. This calls forth attempts to adjust the functioning of the primary system. These attempts challenge the goals of the power group. They thus aim at influencing the first, or volitative, premises for the actions of the decision-makers. These last are being asked to adjust their goals so that the actions deemed necessary to achieve them no longer have the consequences thought undesirable (by the agents in the secondary system). Whether the agents in the primary system will respond to the orders from the secondary system is contingent, just as it is contingent whether the information passing from the primary system will influence the cognitive attitudes of the agents in the secondary system. But once the premises, *i.e.* the volitions of agents in the one and the cognitions of agents in the other system, have been formed the actions which follow become, in the light of the new premises, *logically necessary*.

A student of logic in the tradition of Aristotle, Leibniz, Frege, and the authors of *Principia Mathematica* is likely to find hegelian logic, if he is ever confronted with it, either unintelligible or plainly mistaken. Hegelian logic is also that of orthodox marxism. One of its peculiarities is the vehement rejection of the so-called Law of Double Negation which says that the negation of the negation of a proposition equals that proposition. The hegelians and marxists insist that the negation of the negation—an idea which plays a great role in their writings—leads to something different from the basis of the operation. What do they mean? I shall suggest that we can in *some* cases understand it if we examine their examples and reformulate their ideas in the light of the notion of negative feedback. This *is* a sort of "double negation" process. The cause-factor of the secondary system "denies" the effect which the cause-factor of the primary system brings forth; and the effect of the secondary system "denies" the operations of the cause-factor of the primary system, *i.e.* corrects it so as to "quiet" the first denial. This is a somewhat fanciful description of a process whose logical structure constitutes an interesting object for exact logical analysis. One cannot congratulate Hegel or Marx or Engels for having succeeded with the analysis. But one may with some justification credit them with having anticipated ideas which have later turned out to be of fundamental importance to both the life and the social sciences.[17] I think that several of the key ideas of hegelian and marxist philosophy could be interestingly translated into modern cybernetic and systems-theoretic terminology. The translation would make these ideas more intelligible and precise, and also more accessible to a larger research community than that confined in the windowless chambers of orthodox marxism.[18]

9. In the last two sections of this chapter I shall briefly discuss some problems relating to the question of determinism in history and in the development of society. One of the problems here is to see what "determinism" could mean in these contexts—and to distinguish between kinds of determinism.

It has been one of the main tenets of this work that one

ought to separate, as being utterly distinct, causation in nature and causation, if we are to use that name, in the realm of individual or collective human action. In the light of this distinction many beliefs and ideas concerning determinism in the history of individuals and societies will be seen to be due to conceptual confusion and false analogies between events in nature and intentional action. But even when the mists have dispersed, serious problems remain.

It is useful to distinguish between two types of determinism which can be, and have been, maintained and defended by researchers in these fields. The one is connected with ideas of *predictability*, the other with ideas of *intelligibility* of the historical and social process. Perhaps one could call the types predetermination and post-determination. The intelligibility of history is a determinism *ex post facto*.

One can also make a distinction, both in the physical sciences and the sciences of man, between determinism on the micro-level and on the macro-level.[19] We can often predict with great accuracy and a high degree of reliability the outcome of a process in which a great number of "elements" participate whose individual contributions may be highly unpredictable or completely out of our control. Similarly, one sometimes clearly sees the necessity of some "big event" in history, such as a revolution or a war, and at the same time admits, in retrospect, that the way it happened might have been completely different in detail from what it actually was.[20]

Claims concerning determinism in history and social science, whether of the predictability or of the intelligibility type, have usually been restricted to events on the macro-level. This is true particularly of the predictability claims.[21]

The prototype case of prediction of macro-events with high degree certainty is the prediction of the relative frequencies with which the results in individual performances of an experiment will occur in a mass-experiment. Philosophers have sometimes wanted to see behind this kind of predictability of events the operation of a natural law called the Law of Great Numbers or of the Canceling out of Chance (*Ausgleich des Zufalls*). In the history of the social sciences too, ideas associated with this law have played a not inconsiderable role. The law has been thought somehow to reconcile indeterminism in the behavior of the individual with determinism in the behavior of the collectivity.[22]

The philosophic problems connected with the idea of the *Ausgleich des Zufalls* are of basic importance to the theory of induction and of probability.[23] A detailed discussion of them is out of place here. A few remarks will suffice.

The application of a "law of great numbers" presupposes that probability-values are hypothetically assigned to events which may occur or fail to occur on generically identifiable, repeated occasions for their occurrence. On this hypothetical basis it is calculated that, with a probability so high that we regard it as a "practical certainty," a certain thing will be the case, when the events in question have had a certain number of opportunities to materialize. The predicted thing is normally that a relative frequency will be very near a certain mean value. If nevertheless the practically certain thing does not come true, we either speak of a strange coincidence of chance, or we let the failure recoil on the initial hypotheses of probability-values. The *Ausgleich des Zufalls* is thus a logical consequence of the way we adjust our hypothetical assignments of probabilities to events in the light of statistical experience. There is no "natural law" whose operations would guarantee the *Ausgleich*. And there is no "mysticism" about a reconciliation of individual freedom with collective determinism here.

The question may now be raised of whether there is an analogy in the world of men and societies to these operations of chance in mass-experiments. Records over a long period of time show, for example, a stable rate of suicide within a community. Perhaps, if we predict that about m men in the society will kill themselves within the next twelve months, we can feel confident of the prediction. One can improve upon the analogy with chance events here by "distributing" the suicide rate over the individuals so that we are entitled to speak of the probability that an individual man, randomly selected, will kill himself in the course of the next twelve months. For some purposes this would be a useful operation. But inasmuch as it abstracts from individual differences between men, the picture which it gives of reality is *blurred*. Any (statistical) probability statement can aptly be compared to a blurred picture or said to be, in a characteristic sense, an *incomplete description* of a case.[24]

A social scientist may further explain the difference in suicide rates of two societies as being due to a difference in some features characteristic of the life in them. For example, to a difference in unemployment rates or in the stress under which people work. He may also predict changes in suicide rate consequent upon changes in the ways of living.

This is all very similar to explanation and prediction in the natural sciences, particularly in those where probabilistic concepts and statistical tools play a prominent role. Philosophers of a positivist turn of mind would say that this testifies to the basic methodological unity of all pursuit of knowledge which advances beyond the descriptive stage to the level of laws and uniformities. And some researchers into social phenomena would perhaps claim that *this* is what gives their endeavors the status of a "science."

Explanation and Understanding

I think we can accept all this, but with two important reservations. The first is that this picture shows only a facet of what is going on in social studies—a facet, moreover, which can be said to distinguish them from historical study proper. (But one should not attempt to draw the border sharply here.) The second reservation is that the explanatory patterns which are valid in the micro-world of acting individuals under the macro-level of statistically correlated generic features—say between stress and suicide rate or between economic status and voting behavior—are very different from the patterns of causal explanation which apply in the micro-world of individual events in nature. The difference, briefly, is this:

The systems ("fragments of the history of a world") which experimental science studies can be manipulated by an outside agent. This agent has learnt to reproduce the initial states of the systems under conditions where they would not otherwise originate. From repeated observations he then gets to know the possibilities of development inherent in the system. The systems which social scientists study cannot, as a rule, be manipulated by outside agents. Instead they can be manipulated by agents inside. This means that predictions about the systems' development can, within the limits of human "know how," be made to come true, but can also be made to come false. It is this difference, among others, between prediction in the world of natural events and in the world of agents which philosophers like Karl Popper and Isaiah Berlin have rightly emphasized in their polemics against what the former calls *historicism*.[25] But I am not certain whether they, or for that matter the "historicists" themselves, have not sometimes mistaken the claims of a determinism of the predictability type for the claims of a determinism of a quite different nature.[26]

10. If an action can be explained teleologically, it is in a sense determined, *viz.* determined by certain intentions and cognitive attitudes of men. If every action had a teleological explanation, a *kind* of universal determinism would reign in history and the life of societies.

It seems quite clear that all behavior of *individuals* can*not* be teleologically explained. Some behavior is not intentional at all. But this type of behavior is not of much interest to history or social science either. Perhaps it could be ruled out from consideration altogether in these fields. On the other hand, intentionalistically understood behavior cannot without exception be teleologically explained as the outcome of a practical argument. Intentional action, it seems, can result from completely gratuitous choices. (Cf. above, Ch. III, Sect. 5.) Action conforming to the requirements of custom and norm can usually be linked with a teleological background. (Otherwise "normative pressure" would not be the important force which it is in the life of communities.) But in most cases this teleological background serves only as a "remote" explanatory basis for the actions in the individual cases.

One could say that behavior which is not understood as action has not, or not yet, a place among the recognized *facts* of history or social science. Where individual behavior is concerned, the problem of interpreting it as an action of some sort (as distinct from sheer "reflexes") is seldom, if ever, relevant to historical or social research. *What* the agents do is usually taken for granted in the description we give of their behavior. But with regard to group behavior the case is different. Here the question of *what* the group does, when the individuals who compose it are observed doing certain things, is always pertinent and often problematic. (Cf. above, Sect. 1.) To answer this question constitutes *ipso facto* a kind of explanation. In order to qualify as *fact*, one could say, the material at hand must already have passed a test of explicability.[27]

The determinism which intentionalist understanding and teleological explanation represent could be called a form of *rationalism*. The idea that all action is teleologically explicable would mean an extreme rationalism of a sort. Many proponents of so-called determinism in the classical free-will controversy have, in fact, advocated this sort of rationalist understanding of (free) action. Some of them have maintained that a determinist position, far from undermining the idea of (moral) responsibility, is on the contrary needed in order to account for it properly.[28] This, I think, is basically true. The imputation of responsibility is an imputation of intention(ality) and potential awareness of the consequences of one's actions. It is false, however, to assimilate this case to the determinism of causal necessitation. Again, any claim that human action is always, in this rationalist-teleological sense, determined, would also be false.

From the relativistic rationalism which views actions in the light of set purposes and cognitive attitudes of agents must be distinguished an absolute rationalism which attributes a goal to history or the social process as a whole. This goal can be thought of as something immanent, as I think we have to understand Hegel's notion of the objective and the absolute mind (*Geist*). Or it can be something transcendental, like various models of world-explanation offered by Christian theology. It can perhaps aim at a combination of both types of view. But all such ideas transcend the boundaries of an empirical study of man and society, and therefore also of anything which could reasonably claim to be a "science" in the broader sense of the German word *Wissenschaft*. They may nevertheless be of great interest and value. A teleological interpretation of history and society can influence men in a variety of ways. An interpretation in terms of immanent or transcendental aims can make us acquiesce in things as they happen, thinking that they serve a purpose unknown to us. Or it can urge us to action for ends purported to be set, not by the contingent wills of individual agents, but by the very nature of things or by the will of God.

Notes

I. Two Traditions

1. Nearly all "revolutions" in science testify to the inseparability of the discovery of new facts from the invention of a new theory to explain them—and also to the close interrelation of the description of facts and the formation of concepts. See, for example, the account given in Kuhn 1962, p. 56 and *passim*, of the discovery of oxygen and the overthrow of the phlogiston theory of combustion.

2. Cf. Popper 1935, Sect. 12; Hempel 1942, Sect. 4; Caws 1965, Sect. 13.

3. The thesis of "the structural identity of explanation and prediction" has been criticized by several recent writers. The discussion received decisive impetus from Scheffler 1957 and Hanson 1959. The pros and cons of the thesis are skillfully dissected in Hempel 1965, Sect. 2. 4. For a defense of the thesis see also Angel 1967.

4. The *loci classici* of the confrontation between the "aristotelian" and the "galilean" points of view are Galileo's two works in dialogue form, *Dialoghi sui massimi sistemi tolemaico e copernicano* and *Discorsi e dimostrazioni matematiche intorno à due-*

nuove scienze. It goes without saying that they do not give a historically faithful picture of aristotelian science and its methodology. But they picture with admirable clarity two different approaches to the explanation and understanding of natural phenomena. An excellent review of the contrast between the two types of science is Lewin 1930/1931: "Bei der Gegenüberstellung der aristotelischen und galileischen Begriffsbildung in der Physik kommt es uns naturgemäss weniger auf die persöhnlichen Nüancen der Theorie bei Galilei und Aristoteles an als auf einige ziemlich massive Unterschiede der Denkweise, die für die tatsächliche Forschung der aristotelisch-mittelalterlichen und der nachgalileischen Physik massgebend waren" (p. 423).

5. On the platonic background of the new science of nature which was born in the late Renaissance and the Baroque, see Burtt 1924, Cassirer 1946, and Koyré 1939.

6. These terms give at best only a partial characterization of the contrast. Although there is strong emphasis on teleology in Aristotle and in "aristotelian" science, by no means all explanations characteristic of their way of thinking are teleological. Aristotelian explanations, including many of the notorious cases, were often in terms of "faculties" or "powers" associated with the "essence" of some stuff. Such explanations, however, may be said to *resemble* genuine teleological ones in that they are explications of concepts rather than hypotheses about causes. Similarly, the explanations which Galileo and the "new science" substituted for those of aristotelian science were far from always causal in a strict sense. The prototypes of galilean explanations are in terms of laws connecting phenomena which are numerically measurable determinates of different generic determinables. They are thus explanations conforming to a subsumption-theoretic pattern (see below, Sects. 2 and 5). In this they *differ*, according to the standpoint taken in the present work, from explanations which are genuinely teleological.

7. The term "mechanistic" must be used with caution. Cybernetic and systems-theoretic explanations which conform to subsumption-theoretic patterns (see below, Sect. 7) can be called, in a wide sense, "mechanistic." But they can also be significantly

distinguished from explanations which, in a narrower sense, carry this label.

8. Cf. Mill 1865 and the references to Comte and positivism in Mill 1843, especially in Bk. VI.

9. There are different ways of characterizing "positivism." One characterization links positivism with a phenomenalist or sensualist theory of knowledge, and modern positivism with a verificationist theory of meaning. Another characterization links it with a "scientistic" and "technological" view of knowledge and its uses. Mill is more of a positivist in the first sense than is Comte. Comte's positivism is above all a philosophy of science. (See Comte 1830, "Avertissement de l'Auteur.") His ultimate ambition ("premier but," "but spécial") was to be a champion of the "positive," scientific spirit in the study of social phenomena. (Comte 1830, Leçon I, Sect. 6.) With this he combined a firm belief in the usefulness of scientific knowledge for social reform. "Une . . . propriété fondamentale . . . dans ce que j'ai appelé la philosophie positive, et qui doit sans doute lui mériter plus que toute autre l'attention générale, puisqu'elle est aujourd'hui la plus importante pour la pratique, c'est qu'elle peut être considérée comme le seul base solide de la réorganisation sociale." (Comte 1830, Leçon I, Sect. 8.) As a missionary of a technological attitude to knowledge Comte can, not uninterestingly, be compared to Francis Bacon. Both contributed greatly to the creation of a certain "scientistic climate of opinion," but next to nothing to the actual progress of science.

10. Comte 1830, "Avertissement": ". . . par *philosophie positive* . . . j'entends seulement l'étude propre des généralités des différentes sciences, conçues comme soumises à une méthode unique et comme formant les différentes parties d'un plan général de recherches." Comte 1830, Leçon I, Sect. 10: "Quant à la doctrine, il n'est pas nécessaire qu'elle soit une, il suffit qu'elle soit homogène. C'est donc sous le double point de vue de l'unité des méthodes et de l'homogénéité des doctrines que nous considérons, dans ce cours, les différentes classes de théories positives."

11. Comte 1830, Leçon I, Sect. 6 (on the notion of a "physique sociale") and Leçon II, Sect. 11.

12. Mill 1843, Bk. III, Ch. xii; Comte 1830, Leçon I, Sects. 4 and 24. Comte does not give any systematic account of explanation. His main emphasis is on prediction. Cf. Comte 1844, Pt. I, Sect. 3: "Ainsi, le véritable esprit positive consiste surtout *à voir pour prévoir*, à étudier ce qui est afin d'en conclure ce qui sera, d'aprés le dogme général de l'invariabilité des lois naturelles."

13. Mill 1843, Bk. III, Ch. xii, Sect. 1: "An individual fact is said to be explained, by pointing out its cause, that is, by stating the law or laws of causation, of which its production is an instance." Comte repudiated the search for "causes." He associated it with the "pre-positivist," metaphysical stage in the development of science. In positivist science the role of causes is taken over by general laws. Cf. Comte 1830, Leçon I, Sect. 4, and Comte 1844, Pt. I, Sect. 3.

14. Cf. the quotation from Mill in n. 13 above. Comte 1830, Leçon I, Sect. 2: "L'explication des faits . . . n'est plus désormais que la liaison établie entre les divers phénomènes particuliers et quelques faits généraux."

15. Mill 1843, Bk. VI, Ch. iii, Sect. 2: "The science of Human Nature may be said to exist, in proportion as the approximate truths, which compose a practical knowledge of mankind, can be exhibited as corollaries from the universal laws of human nature on which they rest."

16. Cf. Comte 1844, Pt. I, Sect. 6.

17. Comte, in particular, was conscious of this link with tradition. Cf. Comte 1830, Leçon I, Sect. 5. According to Comte, it was with Bacon and Galileo that science definitely entered the positive stage.

18. Windelband 1894.

19. Droysen 1858. The methodological distinction made by Droysen originally had the form of a trichotomy: the philosophical method, the physical method, and the historical method. The aims of the three methods are, respectively, to know (*erkennen*), to explain, and to understand. On Droysen's hermeneutic methodology of history see Wach 1926/1933, Vol. III, Ch. ii.

20. See Dilthey 1883; 1894; 1900; 1910. On Dilthey's hermeneutics see Stein 1913. On the history of the concept of "Verstehen" generally see Apel 1955.

Chapter I

21. The work which introduced the term *Geisteswissenschaft* appears to have been the translation of Mill's *Logic* by Schiel in 1863. Bk. VI of Mill 1843 is called in the translation "Von der Logik der Geisteswissenschaften oder moralischen Wissenschaften." It was Dilthey who made the term current. Cf. Frischeisen-Köhler 1912.

22. Simmel's psychologistic theory of understanding and of historical knowledge is expounded in Simmel 1892, particularly Ch. I, and Simmel 1918.

23. Droysen 1857/1937, p. 25, had already said: "Unser historisches Verstehen ist ganz dasselbe, wie wir den mit uns Sprechenden verstehen." Dilthey's notion of understanding (Dilthey 1883 and 1894) was originally strongly "psychologistic" and "subjectivist." Later (in Dilthey 1910), apparently under increasing influence from Hegel, he insisted on the "objective" character of the achievements of the understanding method. See also Dilthey 1900, particularly the Appendix, pp. 332–338.

24. The term "sociology" is also used in Mill 1843.

25. The methodological standpoint of Durkheim is best studied in Durkheim 1893 and 1894. His positivist attitude notwithstanding, some of Durkheim's chief ideas, for example those concerning the "représentations collectives" of the social consciousness, could be profitably reinterpreted, I think, in the terms of a hermeneutic methodology of understanding.

26. On Weber's position see in particular Weber 1913 and Weber 1921, Pt. I, Ch. i.

27. Marx shows a marked ambivalence between a "causalist," "scientistic" orientation on the one hand and a "hermeneutic-dialectical," "teleological" on the other hand. This ambivalence, by the way, invites radically different interpretations of his philosophic message. In this regard Marx can, not uninterestingly, be compared to Freud, in whose work an explicit natural-science oriented search for causal explanations often thwarts an implicit hermeneutic and teleological tendency of the thought. With both writers one has the impression that their thinking was to some extent fettered and distorted by the dominant "galileanism" of both the science and the philosophy of science (positivism) of their time.

28. For Hegel on necessity and law see Hegel 1812/1816, Bk. II, Sect. i, Ch. 3 ("Der Grund") and Hegel 1830, Sects. 147–159. Hegel's views of causality, necessity, and explanation are perhaps best studied in the early manuscript known as the *Jenenser Logik*, pp. 40–76. On the concepts of law and necessity in marxist philosophy see Rapp 1968. Marx often spoke of social laws as having an "iron necessity" or of working with "the inexorability of laws of nature." Cf. Marcuse 1941, pp. 317f., and Kon 1964, Vol. I, p. 290. See also the chapter on causality and necessity in nature in Lenin 1909.

29. This schema, often associated with Hegel, is an invention of Fichte. Hegel does not employ it explicitly, but it can rightly be said to *apply* to a great many of the characteristically hegelian, and also marxist, "moves of thought."

30. Cf. Litt 1953, pp. 220ff. ("Evolution und Dialektik").

31. Cf. Hartmann 1923 and Marcuse 1941, pp. 40f. and p. 122.

32. For Hegel on teleology see Hegel 1812/1816, Bk. II, Sect. iii, Ch. 2. "Mechanistic" explanation does not give us *full* understanding of the phenomena of nature; the explanation is completed only when set in a teleological perspective. The "aristotelian" and teleological character of Hegel's and Marx's ideas on law and necessity is emphasized and well documented in Wilenius 1967. I am indebted to its author for help in my own efforts to understand hegelian and marxist thinking. On the teleology implicit in marxism, see also Ch. Taylor 1966.

33. The question of the relation of Dilthey, and the philosophers of the hermeneutic methodology generally, to Hegel is complex. Dilthey's development from a more "subjectivist-psychologistic" towards a more "objectivist-hermeneutic" position was at the same time an increased orientation towards Hegel and the hegelian tradition. (Cf. above n. 23.) On these connections see Marcuse 1932, especially pp. 363ff., and Gadamer 1960, especially Pt. II, Sect. 2. Of decisive importance to the revival of interest in Hegel in this century was Dilthey 1905.

34. A characteristic representative of these latter-day heirs to positivism is Karl Popper. He was always strongly critical of the positivism of the Vienna Circle and of the "inductivism" of a

certain type of positivist philosophy of science. But the somewhat patricidal antipositivism of Popper and his followers must not be allowed to obscure the historic continuity here nor to blur the contrasts with other professedly antipositivist currents of contemporary philosophy. Essentially, the movement of thought sometimes called *critical rationalism* is an upholder in our era of an intellectual tradition whose two great classics are Comte and Mill. Cf. Albert 1968.

35. By Karl Popper, for example, in Popper 1935, Sect. 12. Later, Popper claimed, against Hempel, to be the originator of this very theory of what he calls "causal explanation" (Popper 1945, Ch. XXV, Sect. 2). In point of fact the "Popper-Hempel" theory of explanation had been something of a philosophic commonplace ever since the days of Mill and Jevons. Cf. Ducasse 1925, p. 150f.: "Explanation essentially consists in the offering of a hypothesis of fact, standing to the fact to be explained as case of antecedent to case of consequent of some already known law of connection"; Hobart 1930, p. 300: "To explain an event is to show that it had to happen as it did. That means to exhibit it as the effect of a cause, in other words as a case of a law." Examples could easily be multiplied.

36. Dray 1957, p. 1.

37. Hempel's chief contributions to explanation theory, beginning with the 1942 paper on general laws in history, are collected in Hempel 1965. Noteworthy also is Hempel 1962/1966.

38. The distinction between the two types of explanation model was, as far as I know, first made in Hempel 1959. He later elaborated it in Hempel 1962; 1962/1966; and 1965. Hempel's account of the second model has undergone changes which can be studied in the papers referred to. His terminology has also vacillated. Hempel variously calls explanation not of the deductive type "inductive," "statistical," "probabilistic," and "inductive-statistical."

39. Both the terminology and the meanings of the various terms vacillate. I prefer the pair of terms *explanans* (pl. *explanantia*) and *explanandum*. The first member of the pair is usually defined (understood) so as to include both the basis of the explanation *and* the covering laws. See, *e.g.*, Hempel-Oppenheim 1948, Sect. 2. It

seems to me, largely for terminological reasons, more convenient to use *"explanans"* to mean only the basis, *i.e.* the statements of individual fact from which, in conjunction with the laws, the *explanandum* is deduced.

40. Cf. von Wright 1963a, Ch. II, Sect. 6.

41. The original version of the example which is here paraphrased is in Hempel 1942, Sect. 2. 1.

42. There is no unequivocal standard form of the model (cf. above, n. 38). Our discussion may therefore be said to pertain only to a *version* of the model.

43. Doubts about the explicative efficacy of the model have been raised and discussed in the literature before. See Gluck 1955, Scriven 1959, Dray 1963. The points made by Scriven and Dray are related to the criticism of the model given in the text. Inductive-probabilistic explanations, to use Scriven's happy phrase, "abandon the hold on the individual case" (p. 467). "An event," Scriven says, "can rattle around inside a network of statistical laws, but is located and explained by being so located in the normic network" (*ib.*).

44. On the distinction between individual and generic events and states, see below, Ch. II, Sect. 4, and von Wright 1963a, Ch. II, Sect. 5.

45. On the role of probability in causal analysis see Suppes 1970. The author defines the notion of cause in probabilistic terms (p. 12). By a *prima facie* cause of an event he understands another event such that the prior probability of the first event is smaller than the probability of the first event given the second. I doubt whether this accords with any common or natural use of "cause" (or *"prima facie* cause"). But I can see no objection to speaking of the *relevance* of (the occurrence of) an event to the probability of (the occurrence of) another event as a kind of "causal" relevance.

46. Hempel always insisted on the distinction. The relation of causal explanation to deductive-nomological explanation generally is discussed in detail in Hempel 1965, pp. 347ff. Mill 1843, Bk. III, Ch. xii, Sect. 1, and Popper 1935, Sect. 12 appear to identify, implicitly, causal explanation with explanation under general laws.

47. N. Hartmann 1951 distinguishes between teleology of *pro-*

cesses, of *forms,* and of *wholes.* Ayala 1970, p. 9, mentions three cases of teleology in biology, *viz.* (*a*) "when the end-state or goal is consciously anticipated by the agent," (*b*) self-regulating systems, (*c*) "structures anatomically and physiologically designed to perform a certain function."

48. For critical comments on the paper see R. Taylor 1950a and 1950b and the rejoinder by Rosenblueth and Wiener 1950.

49. R. Taylor 1950a calls the view of Rosenblueth, Wiener, and Bigelow a "mechanistic" conception of purposefulness. The term "mechanistic" must then, however, be used in a broad sense which I think is better covered by the term "causalistic." Cf. above, n. 7.

50. The authors themselves do not call their approach "causal." They are, on the contrary, anxious to distinguish between causality and their notion of teleology. This seems to me to restrict the term "causal" too much.

51. The authors, strictly speaking, argued for a restriction of the notion of "teleological behaviour" to "purposeful reactions which are controlled by the error of the reaction." "Teleological behaviour thus becomes synonymous with behaviour controlled by negative feedback." (Rosenblueth, Wiener, Bigelow 1943, pp. 23–24.)

52. Braithwaite 1953, Ch. X; Nagel 1961, Ch. XII. Representative selections from both works are reprinted in Canfield (ed.) 1966. Braithwaite expressly takes the view that teleological explanation, both of intentional goal-directed activities and of purposeful behavior generally, is reducible to (forms of) causal explanation. Nagel's attitude to the question of reduction of teleology to causal (nonteleological) explanatory patterns is more guarded. It seems a fair rendering of Nagel's position to say that he considers teleological explanations in *biology* "reducible" to causal explanations. For recent discussions of these problems see Ackermann 1969 and Ayala 1970.

53. On the general and philosophical significance of cybernetics, cf. David 1965, Klaus 1961, Lange 1962, and Wiener 1948.

54. Cf. Lange 1962, Ch. I.

55. Comte 1830, Leçon I, Sect. 10: "Le caractère fondamental

Notes

de la philosophie positive est de regarder tous les phénomènes comme assujettis á des *lois* naturelles invariables."

56. On the notion of logical independence see also Ch. II, Sect. 4, and Ch. III, Sect. 3.

57. It is fairly obvious that the deductive-nomological explanation schema in what may be called its "traditional" form is not an adequate statement of the conditions which an explanation of the deductive-nomological type has to satisfy. Admitting this, however, is not in itself a serious criticism of the subsumption theory of explanation. The adequacy of Hempel's schema and further conditions which may have to be imposed on it are discussed in Eberle, Kaplan, and Montague 1961, Fain 1963, Kim 1963, Ackermann 1965, and Ackermann and Stennes 1966.

58. The position called conventionalism in the philosophy of science is associated, in origin, with the name of Henri Poincaré. The chief source is Poincaré 1902, Chs. V–VII. The position, when carried to the extreme, is best studied, I think, in the works of Hans Cornelius and Hugo Dingler. On conventionalism, see also von Wright 1941/1957, Ch. III.

59. Cf. von Wright 1941/1957, Ch. III, Sect. 4, and von Wright 1951, Ch. VI, Sect. 2.

60. Most representatives of conventionalism have been philosophically akin to positivism. This is true not least of the radical conventionalists. Cf. Ajdukiewicz 1934, Cornelius 1931, Dingler 1931 and 1953.

61. The reintroduction into the modern discussion of the idea of natural necessity, and of the view of laws of nature as principles of necessitation, is chiefly due to William Kneale. See Kneale 1949 and 1961. Significantly, Kneale is a leading authority on the history of modal logic and of logic generally. For discussions of the idea of natural necessity see also Nerlich and Suchting 1967, Popper 1967, and Maxwell 1968.

62. The term "nomic" was suggested by W. E. Johnson: "I should propose that *nomic* (from νόμος, a law) should be substituted for necessary as contrasted with contingent. Thus a nomic proposition is one that expresses a pure law of nature" (Johnson 1921/1924, Pt. I, Ch. ix, Sect. 7). Johnson distinguished non-

logical nomic necessities from universals of facts. The former entail the latter, but not conversely. Johnson's views of laws of nature can be said to anticipate the views of Kneale.

63. On this problem see especially Goodman 1954 (in which Goodman 1947 is reprinted), pp. 17–27, 45f., 73–83, and *passim*.

64. Von Wright 1957.

65. *Ib.,* p. 153.

66. For a general orientation see David 1965. On cybernetics in social science, see Buckley 1967 and Buckley (ed.) 1968; a good survey of cybernetics in law is Losano 1969.

67. A very clear statement with a skillfully argued support of the subsumption-theoretic view of dispositional explanations of actions in terms of motivating reasons is given in Hempel 1965, pp. 469–487.

68. Hempel 1962/1966, p. 107.

69. "If we explain, for example, the first division of Poland in 1772 by pointing out that it could not possibly resist the combined power of Russia, Prussia, and Austria, then we are tacitly using some trivial universal law such as: 'If of two armies which are about equally well armed and led, one has a tremendous superiority in men, then the other never wins.' . . . Such a law might be described as a law of the sociology of military power; but it is too trivial ever to raise a serious problem for the students of sociology, or to arouse their attention" (Popper 1945, Ch. XXV, Sect. 2). This may be true. But would anyone dream of "explaining" the division of Poland in the tacit terms of such a "law of sociology"? It is remarkable how well defenders of the covering law theory of historical explanation succeed in evading relevant examples.

70. This is Dray's model example. See Dray 1957, pp. 25, 33ff., 51, 97, 102, 134. The example was introduced into the discussion by P. Gardiner. See Gardiner 1952, pp. 67, 87ff. The paraphrase of the example given here has a slightly different twist from the example in the discussions by Dray and Gardiner.

71. Dray 1957, Ch. V. He has later elucidated his position in Dray 1963. Hook (ed.) 1963 contains several contributions to the discussion of Dray's explanation model for action.

72. Dray's explanation model has been criticized by Hempel from

the covering law theorist's point of view, in Hempel 1962 and again in Hempel 1965, Sect. 10.3. A criticism from a standpoint which is essentially sympathetic to Dray's is presented in Donagan 1964. Donagan makes a distinction between actions being *intelligible* and their being *rational*. Dray's choice of term may be somewhat unfortunate. It easily suggests a "rationalist" interpretation of history in some stronger sense than actually intended by Dray himself. (Cf. below, Ch. IV, Sect. 10.) For a critical discussion of Dray's view, see also Louch 1966.

73. On the relations between recent analytic philosophy and the philosophy of *Verstehen*, see Gardiner 1966.

74. This merit it can be said to share with Hampshire 1959.

75. Anscombe 1957, Sect. 33. Neglect of practical reasoning, however, has not been as complete as Miss Anscombe seems to think. Hegel's doctrine of what he occasionally also calls "Schluss des Handelns" is interestingly similar to the idea of a practical syllogism as treated in the present work. In the hegelian practical inference schema the first premise is afforded by the subject's aiming at an end ("der subjektive Zweck"), the second premise is constituted by the contemplated means to the end, and the conclusion consists of the "objectivation" of the aim in action ("der ausgeführte Zweck"). Hegel writes: "Der Zweck schliesst sich durch ein Mittel mit der Objektivität und in dieser mit sich selbst zusammen. . . . Das Mittel ist daher die *formale* Mitte eines *formalen* Schlusses; es ist ein *Äusserliches* gegen das *Extrem* des subjektiven Zweckes so wie daher auch gegen das Extrem des objektiven Zweckes" (Hegel 1812/1816, Bk. II, Sect. iii, Ch. 2 B). I am indebted to Mr. Juha Manninen for these observations on affinities between Aristotle and Hegel.

76. Aristotle, *Ethica Nicomachea* 1147 a 25–30.

77. Anscombe 1957, Sect. 33. The point has since been an object of controversy. Kenny 1966 argues for the *sui generis* character of practical reasoning. Jarvis 1962 argues against it. A mediating position is taken in Wallace 1969.

78. This view will, of course, he contested by those who take what in Ch. III, Sect. 4, below, is called a "causalist" view of the validity of practical arguments.

79. Melden 1961, Kenny 1963, d'Arcy 1963, and Brown 1968, to mention a few of the more important ones.

80. For a defense of the subsumption-theoretic explanation model for actions and of the idea that actions have causes, see Brandt and Kim 1963, Davidson 1963, and Churchland 1970. A "mechanistic" explanation model using cybernetic ideas is proposed in Ackermann 1967. The most recent major work on explanation theory and philosophy of science generally, Stegmüller 1969, is decidedly in the tradition of positivism and logical empiricism. It should also be mentioned that the four papers in the collection Vesey (ed.) 1968 dealing with the problem of actions and causes, *viz.* those by Kolnai, Henderson, Pears, and Whiteley, all defend a causalist view of the motivational mechanism of actions.

81. In Winch 1964a there is an interesting discussion of the applications of his views to social anthropology and the understanding of primitive cultures.

82. Winch 1964b disputes that he is attempting to devise a methodology of the social sciences. This is true, if by methodology one means, roughly, an account of the methods scientists use. But it is not true, if by the term one understands, as we do here, the *philosophy* of method.

83. See the criticism in Louch 1963 and the author's reply, Winch 1964b.

84. Cf. Wilenius 1967, p. 130. A philosopher within the phenomenological mainstream, whose thoughts on the nature of social reality and the methodology of the social sciences have affinities with Winch's, is Alfred Schütz (1899–1959). His book *Der sinnhafte Aufbau der sozialen Welt, eine Einleitung in die verstehende Soziologie* appeared on the eve of the eclipse of culture in Europe and remained strangely neglected, even after the author had found refuge in the United States. Schütz's collected papers in English, including a substantial portion of *Der sinnhafte Aufbau,* have been published posthumously (Schütz 1964).

85. Cf. Yolton 1966, p. 16.

86. The chief source is Gadamer 1960. Perhaps one could, with due caution, distinguish between hermeneutic philosophers of a *dialectic* and those of an *analytic* orientation. The term "hermeneu-

tic philosophy" might then be used as a generic name for both trends. This would serve the purpose of marking a sharper divide than has up to now been thought appropriate between analytic philosophy stemming from the later Wittgenstein and analytic philosophy of the positivist or logical empiricist mainstream. With time, such a regrouping will probably do more justice to the morphology of trends in contemporary thought than placing Wittgensteinian philosophy under the heading "analytic" and regarding continental hermeneutic philosophy as basically a variant of phenomenology.

87. On the place of language in hermeneutic philosophy, see the collection of papers in Gadamer (ed.) 1967. Here should also be mentioned the recent interest in the view of language implicit in Hegel's thinking. See Lauener 1962, Simon 1966, and Derbolav 1970.

88. Originally, the art of interpretation of written documents. On the history of the term and of the movement, see Apel 1966, Dilthey 1900, Gadamer 1960, and Wach 1926/1933.

89. On this affinity, see Apel 1966. On the relation between analytic and hermeneutic philosophy generally, see Apel 1965/1967, Habermas 1967, and Gadamer 1969.

90. Cf. Apel 1965/1967; 1968; and Radnitzky 1968, Vol. II.

91. Radnitzky 1968, Vol. II, pp. 106ff. On the criticism of *Verstehen* and of hermeneutic methodology from the standpoint of analytic philosophy and positivism, see Neurath 1931, p. 56; Hempel 1942, Sect. 6; Hempel-Oppenheim 1948, Pt. I, Sect. 4; Hempel 1965, Sect. 10.3; Abel 1948; Martin 1969.

92. The distinction between the two trends seems first to have been made in Krajewski 1963. See also Kusý 1970.

93. Sources for the study of the impact of cybernetics on marxist dialectical materialism are Klaus 1961 and Kirschenmann 1969.

94. Cf. Klaus 1961, pp. 290–324; Lange 1962.

95. Cf. Krajewski 1963 and Skolimowski 1965.

96. Skolimowski 1965, p. 245.

97. The name appears to have been first suggested by Adam Schaff in Schaff 1961. The views grouped under this heading constitute a very mixed bunch, some being more "orthodox," others

again more "revisionist." See the collection of essays in Fromm (ed.) 1965. See also Marković 1969: "Marxism today really is a whole cluster of opposite orientations and tendencies" (p. 608).

98. The works of Lukács on the young Hegel and the young Marx (Lukács 1948 and 1955) have been of great importance to the hegelian reorientation of marxist philosophy. Lukács 1948 is violently polemical against Dilthey's work of 1905 on the young Hegel, which was crucial to the revival of interest in Hegel early in this century.

99. The Frankfurt School (Horkheimer, Adorno, Fromm, Marcuse, Habermas) may be said to occupy a position at the intersection of hermeneutic philosophy and humanist marxism.

100. Sartre 1960. On Sartre and marxism, see Desan 1965.

II. *Causality and Causal Explanation*

1. See Hume 1739, Bk. I, Pt. iii, Sect. 1 and Sect. 14, and, in particular, Hume 1748, Sect. iv, Pt. 1.

2. Hume 1739, Bk. I, Pt. iii, Sect. 14; Hume 1748, Sect. iv, Pt. 2, and Sect. vii, Pt. 2.

3. For a survey of the efforts to solve "the Problem of Hume" see von Wright 1941/1957.

4. The dictum is by C. D. Broad in Broad 1926.

5. This has been maintained by philosophers as differing in general position as Comte (cf. above, Ch. I, Sect. 2) and Collingwood. Comte 1844, Pt. I, Sect. 3: "La rèvolution fondamentale qui caractérise la virilité de notre intelligence consiste essentiellement à substituer partout, á l'inaccessible détermination des causes proprement dites, la simple recherche des *lois*, c'est-à-dire des relations constantes qui existent entre les phénomènes observés." Comte 1851, Introduction. Collingwood 1940, p. 327. Cf. also Donagan 1962, p. 145.

6. Russell 1912/1913, p. 171.

7. *Ib.*, p. 184.

8. Nagel 1965, p. 12.

9. Suppes 1970, p. 5.

10. Russell 1912/1913 and Campbell 1921, pp. 49–57.

11. Cf. Popper 1935, Sect. 12. The relation between causal explanation and subsumptive explanation of the deductive-nomological type is discussed in detail in Hempel 1965, Sect. 2.2. According to Hempel, *all* causal explanation is deductive-nomological, but not all deductive-nomological explanation is causal.

12. It is useful here to note a distinction between the explanation of *facts,* such as the occurrence of an event, and the "explanation," if we are to call it that, of (scientific) *laws.* In this book I am discussing only the first kind of explanations. According to a common, though hardly uncontestable, view the explanation of laws consists in deriving them from, or in showing that they are special cases of, more general laws. This is deductive-nomological explanation of the subsumption-theoretic type. Cf. Mill 1843, Bk. III, Ch. xiii, and Braithwaite 1953, Ch. XI. "A law or uniformity of nature is said to be explained, when another law or laws are pointed out, of which that law itself is but a case, and from which it could be deduced" (Mill). "To explain a law is to exhibit an established set of hypotheses from which the law follows" (Braithwaite). This, however, is *not* "causal explanation"—at least not in any very good sense of this term. A law should not be said to "cause" another law to be valid, anymore than the truth of $2^n > n$ "causes" 2^3 to be greater than 3.

13. On the distinction between the various condition concepts and the elements of their logic, see von Wright 1951, Ch. III, Sect. 2. On the relation between condition concepts and causal ideas, see also Mackie 1965, Marc-Wogau 1962, Scriven 1964, and Vanquickenborne 1969.

14. On the meaning of "generic" see below, Sect. 4.

15. The pioneer work in this field is Broad 1930. For a fuller treatment see von Wright 1951, Ch. IV. For a summary see von Wright 1941/1957, Ch. IV, Sects. 3–5, of the revised edition.

16. Much confusion in the discussion of causality and in inductive logic has arisen from the failure to keep apart different relations of conditionship. Thus in Hume 1748, Sect. vii, Pt. 2, "cause" is defined, almost in the same breath, first in the sufficient and then in the necessary condition sense—evidently in the belief that the two senses are identical: "We may define a cause to be *an object*

followed by another, and where all the objects similar to the first are followed by objects similar to the second. Or in other words [*sic!*] where, *if the first object had not been, the second never had existed."* Mill 1843 is full of examples of similar confusions. See von Wright 1941/1957, Ch. IV, Sect. 5, and von Wright 1951, Ch. VI, Sect. 4, pp. 158–163.

17. Be it observed that the term "strict implication" is here used in a sense which does *not* commit us to the view that the necessity of the implication is *logical* necessity. A pioneer work in the field of modal, nonextensionalist analysis of causation is Burks 1951.

18. The question, in particular, whether a cause can operate in direction towards the past has been much discussed in recent literature. The current discussion can be said to have started from Dummett 1954 and Flew 1954. Among the more important contributions to it are Black 1955, Chisholm 1960, Chisholm-R. Taylor 1960, Dummett 1964, and Chisholm 1966. For a bibliography see Gale (ed.) 1968.

19. On the notion of an occasion and on the distinction between generic and individual proposition-like entities see von Wright 1963a, Ch. II, Sect. 4.

20. For a detailed presentation of this system of tense-logic or Logic of Change see von Wright 1965; 1969.

21. For a more detailed presentation see von Wright 1968b.

22. According to a standard definition, a system is a class of elements with a coordinated set of relations. See Hall and Fagen 1956, p. 81; Lange 1962; Buckley 1967. This conception of a system is much wider than the one discussed here. Our notion of a system is virtually the same as Rescher's notion of a *discrete state system*. See Rescher 1963. It is also related to the cybernetic notion of a *dynamic system*. See Ashby 1952, Ch. 11, and Ashby 1956, Ch. III, Sect. 1 and 11.

23. Important aspects of such considerations are the association of magnitudes of *probability* with the alternative developments at each point and of magnitude of *value* with the total states or worlds.

24. A system which is a fragment of another system will pass through a fewer number of stages. A conditionship relation between

a state at stage m and a state at stage n of the fragment system which holds also for the total system is a relation between a state at stage $m + k$ and a state at stage $n + k$ of the total system, where k is the difference in numbers of stages between the systems. Similarly, a conditionship relation between a state at stage m and a state at stage n of the bigger system is a conditionship relation between the first state at stage $m - k$ and the second state at stage $n - k$ of the fragment system. If $m - k < 1$, then the conditionship relation within the total system has no relation corresponding to it in the fragment system. (This is so since the conditioning state belongs to a stage which is anterior to the initial state of the fragment system.)

25. These questions concerning conditionship relations must not be confused with questions relating to "contingent" or "relative" conditions discussed in Sect. 6.

26. This relativity of the conditionship relations to a system requires for its symbolic expression in the $PL + T + \wedge + M$ calculus the use of *iterated* ("higher order") modal operators. For example, assume that the occurrence of d_1 at the fourth stage is a necessary condition for the appearance of p in e_1. This means that the system's passing through c_1 at the third stage is *sufficient* to ensure that it is *necessary* for the system to go through d_1 at the fourth stage in order to reach an end-state containing p. Let us, for the sake of argument, accept the simplifying assumption that a strict implication is a satisfactory symbolic expression of the fact that its antecedent is a sufficient condition of its consquent, and its consequent a necessary condition of its antecedent. The above relativity of the conditionship relations could then be "read off" from the following formula ·

$$N(c_1 \rightarrow N(tT(tTp) \rightarrow tTd_1)),$$

on the understanding that t signifies an arbitrary tautology.

27. Any system may in its turn be viewed as a fragment of larger systems. Conditionship relations which hold within the first system need not hold within those larger systems.

28. For a general definition of closedness, see Hall and Fagen 1956, p. 86. It is important to note that closedness, as here defined, is a property of a system *on a given instantiation of it, i.e.* on an

occasion when its initial state occurs and the system goes through some of its possible courses of development in a number n of successive stages. The same system which is (occurs) closed on one sequence of occasions for its instantiation, need not be closed on another sequence of occasions.

29. Cf. Nagel 1965, pp. 19ff. The type of case discussed by Nagel is slightly different from the one discussed by us in the text. Nagel is concerned with the "contingent necessity" of a factor. The types of "relative" condition discussed under *ii* and *iii* in the text are *related* to that which Mackie (1965, p. 245) calls an *inus*-condition, *i.e.* an indispensable part of a sufficient condition which is not also a necessary condition. They are further related to what Marc-Wogau (1962, pp. 226f.) calls "a moment in a minimal sufficient and at the same time necessary condition *post factum*" and also to the characterization of causes of particular events given by Scriven (1964, p. 408). The three authors in question try to state conditions which a factor has to satisfy in order to qualify as a "cause," in addition to being a "contingently sufficient condition" in the sense explained in the text. It is not certain that a satisfactory characterization can be given in terms of various conditionship relations alone. One may also have to consider questions of the *manipulability* (control) of the factors (see below, Sects. 7–10) and questions of an *epistemic* nature. The latter concern the order in which the presence of factors becomes known to us or is taken into account in the explanation. The relevance of the epistemic order is reflected in the operation of *extending* initial fragments of systems, either by the inclusion of further elements in the state-space or by considering a greater number of stages in the systems developments.

30. The credit for having first emphasized the important role of explanations which answer questions *how* something or other was *possible* belongs, I think, to William Dray. Explanations of this kind are "no less" subsumption-theoretic than explanations which answer questions *why* something or other happened. (Far from all answers to *Why necessary?* questions are subsumption-theoretic explanations. Cf. below, Ch. IV.) When *How possible?* explanations are subsumption-theoretic, they conform to a covering

law model. But this model is not identical with the original form of
the hempelian schema. The acknowledgment of the independent
logical status of *How possible?* explanations should not be regarded
as a criticism of the hempelian theory of explanation, but rather as
a supplementation of it in an important respect. It is nevertheless
interesting to note that critics of Dray's opinions have tended to
view with suspicion *How possible?* explanations and sometimes
tried to force them into the mould of hempelian *Why necessary?*
explanations. See Dray 1968. Under no circumstances should one
regard the distinction between the two types of explanation as
characterizing a general difference between the explanatory patterns
of the natural and the human sciences.

31. As noted in Ch. I, Sect. 1, n. 3, the question of the relation
between explanation and prediction has been much discussed in
recent literature. This discussion, however, has on the whole only
concerned the predictive powers of answers to *Why?* questions.

32. A notable exception is Ernest Nagel. Many of his analyses of
teleology concern typical cases of "quasi-teleology" and aim at
showing their *causal* character. See Nagel 1953; 1961, especially pp.
401–427; 1965.

33. A good survey of the problem situation in this area is
Lagerspetz 1959. The author's own position is close to that of
Nagel.

34. On this "counterfactual element" involved in the notion of
an action, see below Ch. III, Sect. 10. Cf. also Black 1958, p. 24,
and von Wright 1968c, Ch. II, Sect. 6. My own previous view of
the matter, however, is somewhat different from the position which
I argue here.

35. The phrase "sufficient condition on some occasion" must not
be misunderstood. If *a* is a sufficient condition of *b*, then on *all*
occasions, when *a* is, *b* is too. But it may be the case that, on *some*
occasions of its occurrence, *b* is associated with the sufficient condition *a*, on others with some other of its sufficient conditions, and
on still other occasions with no sufficient condition at all.

36. Jaeger 1934, Bk. I, Ch. 9; Kelsen 1941, Ch. V, called "Die
Entstehung des Kausalgesetzes aus dem Vergeltungsprinzip in der
griechischen Naturphilosophie."

Chapter II

37. Cf. Cohen 1942, p. 13.

38. Beside the phrases "doing things" and "bringing things about" there is also the phrase "making things happen." None of the three phrases, as commonly used, can be unambiguously associated with either member in the pair of concepts which I here, in a technical sense, call the result and the consequence(s) of an action. But it seems to me that "doing" is most naturally associated with the result and "bringing about" with the consequence of an action, whereas "making happen" is more naturally than the other two phrases used ambiguously for either result or consequence. Cf. Black 1958.

39. The distinction between basic and nonbasic actions was introduced into the recent discussion by A. C. Danto. See Danto 1963; 1965a; 1966. The way Danto makes the distinction is open to criticism. Cf. Stoutland 1968. Danto defines a basic action as one which is not caused by any other action by the same agent. Stoutland's definition is slightly different: a basic action of an agent is one which he does not perform by performing some other action. The latter definition is decidedly better; it evades, for one thing, the dubious notion of "causing an action." See also below, Ch. III, n. 38.

40. The idea that action is conceptually prior to cause has a long ancestry in the history of thought. It also has a great many different variants. One of its champions was Thomas Reid. His opinion concerning the priority of the idea of action (active power) to that of causal efficiency is, however, rather different from the view taken here. According to Reid, our idea of *cause* and *effect* in nature is modeled on an *analogy* between the causal relation and that of an *agent* to his *action*. The notion of "active power" in a being, Reid says, is the idea that the being "can do certain things, if he wills" (Reid 1788, Essay I, Ch. V). A view of the relation between the notion of cause and that of action which is more akin to the view taken here is Collingwood's notion of the cause as "handle." Cf. Collingwood 1940, p. 296. The position most similar to mine which I have found in the literature is the one propounded in Gasking 1955. On Gasking's view, "the notion of causation is essentially connected with our manipulative

techniques for producing results" and "a statement about the cause of something is very closely connected with a recipe for producing it or for preventing it" (p. 483). This is substantially true also of the cases when some particular event of a complex and global character, which no one could have produced by manipulation, is said to have caused another particular event. For example, when the rise in mean sea-level at a certain geological epoch is attributed to the melting of the Polar ice-cap. (Cf. our example on p. 70 about the eruption of Vesuvius and the destruction of Pompeii.) For "when one can properly say this sort of thing it is always the case that people can produce events of the first sort as a means to producing events of the second sort" (p. 483). This manipulative notion of cause Gasking calls "the fundamental or primitive one" (p. 486). He makes the observation, which seems to me correct and important, that this notion of a cause does not figure prominently in the theoretical statements of scientists (*ib.*). The progress of natural science can, from one point of view, be said to consist in the transition from "manipulative recipes" to "functional laws" (p. 487). This agrees with the view of Russell and others. But it should then be added that, for purposes of experiments and technical applications, these functional relationships provide a logical basis from which new recipes for producing or preventing things may be extracted. This accounts for the fact, noted by Nagel (cf. above, p. 36), that the notion of ("manipulative") causation continues to be "pervasive in the accounts natural scientists give of their laboratory procedures."

41. For a forceful defense of the humean, "passivist," regular sequence view of causation and natural law see Hobart 1930. The author says that "mere sequence in events themselves generates necessity in them as characterized by us" (p. 298). *In a sense* this is also true of the view of causation which I am defending here. The idea of natural necessity, as I see it, is rooted in the idea that we can bring about things by doing other things. Our knowledge that things done "bring about" other things rests, however, on observations of regular sequences. To say that things "bring about" other things is therefore misleading: *this* "bringing about" is nothing but regular sequence. Our knowledge that we can do things,

Chapter II

moreover, rests on our assurance that certain states of affairs will stay unchanged (or will change in a certain way), unless we interfere, productively or preventively, with the course of nature. Whence have we got this assurance? Obviously from experience. So, in the last resort the notion of action is rooted in our familiarity with empirical regularities.

42. Simon 1953 defends a related view of the problem of the asymmetry of the causal relation. He rejects the idea that "cause could be defined as functional relationship in conjunction with sequence in time" (p. 159). The asymmetry of the relation must, according to him, be accounted for in the terms of power to control and intervene with the structure of a model.

43. The crude model or picture which we are using here does not, of course, claim to be realistic. "Brain events" are not even "in principle" open to ocular inspection. From the point of view of the present discussion, the crude model performs its logical function, *if* it is admitted that brain events are neural processes which can be defined and identified *independently* of the effects which they produce on the processes called "muscular activity." Whether this condition of independence is in fact satisfied I am not competent to judge. I am not aware that it has ever been questioned. But the matter might be well worth inquiring into.

44. The idea that an agent can bring about brain events "in the past" is discussed, most interestingly, in Chisholm 1966. According to Chisholm, an agent by doing something, *e.g.* raising his arm, makes certain brain events happen. A causal relation of this type, *viz.* between an agent and an event in the world, Chisholm calls *immanent.* He distinguishes this from causal relations which he calls *transeunt* and which are between an event and another event. The relation between the rising of the arm and the (antecedent) brain events is thus transeunt causation. Using Chisholm's distinction, one could say that I am here arguing for the existence of instances of transeunt causation operating towards the past. For I try to argue that it is the rising of my arm which "causes" certain anterior brain events to take place. Chisholm's notion of "immanent causation" seems to me connected with insurmountable difficulties. Chisholm says that "the nature of transeunt causation

is no more clear than is that of immanent causation" (p. 22). In a sense I can agree with him. And perhaps one could say that *my* notion of "(transeunt) causation," because of its dependence on the notion of action, has *a* notion of "immanent causation" already built in. Chisholm also says that "if we did not understand the concept of immanent causation, we would not understand that of transeunt causation" (p. 22). Here my position seems to come very close to his. If for the words "immanent causation" we substitute "action" we get my version of the thought. One could, if one wished, *call* action "immanent causation" and thus give this phrase a meaning. But I do not think the notion of immanent causation can be employed to *elucidate* the concept of an action.

III. *Intentionality and Teleological Explanation*

1. This difference between the types of explanation would be a difference "on the surface" only, if teleological and quasi-causal explanations turned out to be transformable into (genuinely) causal explanations. It would then still be true that the explanation, *e.g.*, of the running of the man who is anxious to catch the train, does not depend for its correctness on the truth of the assumed nomic connection between running and arrival at the station in time for the train. But it would depend on the truth of a nomic connection between his "anxiety to catch the train" (interpreted perhaps as some global state of his brain and body) and his running.

2. This would correspond, I think, to the view taken in Braithwaite 1953, pp. 322–341; in Hempel 1959, Sect. 7; and in Nagel 1961, pp. 401–428. As Nagel puts it: "Every statement about the subject matter of a teleological explanation can in principle be rendered in nonteleological language, so that such explanations together with all assertions about the contexts of their use are translatable into logically equivalent nonteleological formulations" (p. 421). This agrees with the view of "radical cyberneticism" in the sense, for example, of Klaus 1961, pp. 290–325.

3. I do not wish to minimize the importance of the prospects which cybernetics have opened for an analysis of teleology in causal

terms. This analysis, for one thing, has helped us to distinguish more clearly between *types* of teleology. My claim is *not* that the explanation of goal-directed behavior and purposefulness cannot sometimes (often) be reduced to conformity with the covering law model. My claim is only that this reduction does not apply to *all* forms of teleology. I should have no quarrel with those who preferred to call the nonreducible forms by some other name, *e.g.* intentionality, and reserve the name teleology for the reducible forms.

4. It would be inconvenient and pedantic to object to the use of the word "cause" for other than instantiations of nomic connections. But it seems to me sensible to object to the use of the technical term "causal explanation" for explanations which do not conform to a subsumption-theoretic pattern.

5. See Mayr 1965 and Ayala 1970.

6. An alternative name for explanations relying on nomic ties between the *explanandum* and some posterior *explanantia* would be "terminal causation." It was coined by the Finnish philosopher Kaila (1956). He contrasted *terminal* with *initial* causation. It was Kaila's opinion that terminal causation was of great importance, not only in the life and behavioral sciences, but also in physics— and that the role of causal explanations in the terms of antecedent conditioning factors had been much exaggerated.

7. Cf. Collingwood 1946, p. 213, where an act is described as "the unity of the outside and inside of an event."

8. By "behaviorism" one usually understands a doctrine or method which accounts for the behavior of organisms in terms of stimulus and response. It is striking, however, that in the *clear* cases of unconditioned or conditioned reflexes it is not quite natural to speak of "behavior" (of the stimulated and reacting organism). Salivation, or the jerking of a knee, are reactions to stimuli. But only people who have had their talk perverted by behaviorist jargon would think it natural to call such reactions "behavior" of a dog or a man. (But one could call them behavior of certain glands or of a knee.) The interesting, and controversial, part of the behaviorist thesis could therefore be said to be the claim that behavior *too* can be explained "behavioristically," as (complicated forms of) responses to stimuli. I think observations like these are useful be-

cause they draw attention to conceptual differences and warn us against overhasty generalizations. It is not my desire to protest against established technical terminology in psychological research. On the notion of behavior and the related concepts of act(ion) and movement, see the interesting paper by D. W. Hamlyn (1953).

9. It might be useful to mark a distinction between *logical* and *causal* consequence(s). When we speak of the consequences of an opinion, statement, or proposition we usually mean logical consequences. But when used in connection with action the term nearly always refers to causal consequences.

10. Compare the example of the pumping man in Anscombe 1957, Sects. 23–26.

11. For a fuller treatment of the formal logic of action concepts see von Wright 1963a and 1968c.

12. Muscular activity is caused by neural activity. Proponents of the view which I am here sketching would therefore often say that the immediate effect of the will is some neural event which would then presumably be regarded as the immediate outer aspect of the action. Cf. Pritchard 1945, p. 193: "Where we have willed some movement of our body and think we have caused it, we cannot have directly caused it. For what we directly caused, if anything, must have been some change in our brain." Neural events, however, do not qualify as that which I here call the immediate outer aspect of an action. This is because they are not the *results* of *basic* actions. (See Ch. II, Sect. 8.) They belong, if at all, to the outer aspects of actions only as *consequences* of the results of certain basic actions. (Cf. the discussion of possible retroactive causation in Ch. II, Sect. 10.) If we construe the argument about the will as a cause of action in such a way that the will is being said to cause neural events which, in turn, cause some molar behavior, then we may be said to use the neural states as a "wedge" to separate the inner and the outer aspect of an action. The alleged necessity of this separation, in my opinion, only serves to illustrate the conceptually unsound nature of a "causal theory of action."

13. For Hume's insistence on independence of cause and effect

Chapter III

see particularly Hume 1738, Bk. I, Pt. iii, Sect. 6. Also if one takes the view that causal connections are a species of natural necessity, one would wish to maintain that cause and effect must be *logically* independent.

14. This position has been championed, most forcefully, by A. I. Melden and by a number of authors writing under his influence. Cf. Melden 1961, p. 53: "The interior event which we call 'the act of volition' . . . must be logically distinct from the alleged effect—this surely is one of the lessons we can derive from a reading of Hume's discussion of causation. Yet nothing can be an act of volition that is not logically connected with what is willed—the act of willing is intelligible only as the act of willing whatever it is that is willed."

15. For a lucid discussion of the argument with good critical observations see Stoutland 1970.

16. Thus, for example, in Melden 1961, as seen from the quotation above in n. 14, in Daveney 1966, or White 1967. Cf. also Wittgenstein 1967a, Sects. 53–60.

17. Cf. Stoutland 1970, p. 125. The author quite rightly points out that the view which makes "the objects of intentions part of the internal structure of intentions" in no way contradicts the possibility (statement) that "there is a contingent relation between intentions and the occurrence of what fulfills them."

18. In order to show that two singular propositions, p and q, are not logically independent one has to show that at least one of the four combinations, $p\&q$, $p\&\sim q$, $\sim p\&q$, and $\sim p\&\sim q$, is a logical impossibility. The mere fact that it is logically impossible to verify, or falsify, the one proposition without also verifying, or falsifying, the other does not entail that the two propositions are logically independent. Only in combination with the further thesis that it must be *logically* possible to come to know the truth-value of, *i.e.* to verify or falsify, any singular contingent proposition does it follow that the propositions are independent. I consider this view of the relation of verifiability and propositional meaning acceptable, but I shall not argue for it here.

19. The possibility that *intentions* function as causes is expressly the object of discussion in Ch. Taylor 1964, Daveney 1966, and

Notes

Malcolm 1968. Taylor says (p. 33) that intentions "bring about" behavior. But he also denies (*ib.*) that the intention is "a causal antecedent" of the intended behavior. Taylor uses "cause" to mean what is here called a humean cause. But, as Malcolm (p. 59f.) observes, "cause" also has a wider use. Malcolm distinguishes (*ib.*) between intentions in an action and previously formed intentions to do a certain thing. The first are in no sense causes, he says. The second bring about behavior and thus function as causes, although not, if I understand Malcolm correctly, as humean causes. For a discussion of Malcolm's position see Iseminger 1969.

20. This role of behavioral uniformities is rightly emphasized in MacIntyre 1966. But the author, it seems to me, uncritically interprets the uniformities as "causal laws." The fact, for example, that defeat at cards (regularly) makes a person angry is hardly "a perfect example of humean causation" (*ib.*, p. 222), although the bodily states accompanying and characteristic of anger may have humean causes. Cf. below, Ch. IV, Sect. 5, on stimulus and response and mechanisms of "making people do things."

21. The type of argument which is here called a "practical inference" is different from that studied in von Wright 1963b. There the conclusion which emerges from the premises was taken to be a norm "A must do *a*." Both types, moreover, are different from the forms of practical, or "orthopractic," reasoning studied in Castañeda 1960/1961 and Rescher 1966. All these types are related, but it seems doubtful whether they have any generic groundform in common. See also above, Ch. I, Sect. 9, and von Wright 1968b.

22. It is a logical feature of practical inferences that their premises and their conclusion should have the characteristic called "referential opacity." This means that one cannot, without restriction, substitute for the descriptions of the states of affairs and results of action which occur in them any other description of identically the same state or result. Action which is intentional under one description of its result need not be so under any other description of it, and a means to an end which under one description is considered necessary need not be considered necessary under another.

196

23. On the conceptual character and conditions of trying, see von Wright 1963a, Ch. III, Sect. 10, and McCormick and Thalberg 1967.

24. In thinking this he may, of course, be mistaken. His mistake will then normally be revealed to him when he sets himself to do the thing. His behavior is perhaps completely unlike anything which would lead to the result wished for. But it may nevertheless be aiming at this end, be "meant" as an effort to reach it.

25. It may be suggested that the conclusion should be formulated as follows: Therefore A (now) sets himself to do *a* no later than at time *t'*. Under this formulation of its conclusion the argument would, I think, indeed be logically conclusive. This is so because to "set" oneself now to do something in the future can hardly mean anything else than that from now on, and for some time, one sticks to the intention and opinion concerning the required action which one has formed. (Cf. what is said in Sect. 8 on changes in intentions and cognitive attitudes.) But this is a different sense of "setting oneself to do" from the one which is here contemplated. (Cf. above, Sect. 4.)

26. I am indebted to Allen Wood for noticing the distinction between forgetting one's intention and forgetting to do the intended thing.

27. Cf. above, n. 18.

28. On the distinction between the two senses of "can do," *viz.* the generic sense which signifies ability and the sense which signifies success on some individual occasion, see von Wright 1963a, Ch. III, Sect. 9.

29. But we may in cases of apparent conflict between the generalization and the individual case prefer to rely on the former for redescribing the latter rather than let an independent description of the individual case overthrow what we think is a reliable generalization (concerning the agent's character, dispositions, or habits). We sometimes say, "This is what he *must* have meant by his behavior, knowing what he is like," although he himself stubbornly, and maybe even in good faith, denies our imputation of intentionality. (Subconscious motives.)

30. To be rescued is not what the agent *intends*. This is something

he *wants*. What he intends is, roughly speaking, to do what he can in order to be rescued. His intention is to create a situation in which it is possible for him to get out of his predicament. It is this intention which impels him to give a truthful answer to the question why he is crying "help!" But it *need not* impel him to this. Whether it does or not depends on the epistemic attitude supplementing his intention. Perhaps he thinks he will be rescued in any case, once he has succeeded in attracting peoples' attention, and that he could now safely risk even lying about his intentions and wants, if questioned.

31. Cf. the "concluding postscript" to Malcolm 1968, p. 72.

32. Cf. Wittgenstein 1953, Sect. 337: "An intention is imbedded in its situation, in human customs and institutions."

33. The genuinely "practical" inference could also be called a *commitment* to action. It is an argument conducted in the first person. Its conclusion, when expressed in words, is "I shall do *a* (now)" or "I shall do *a* no later than at time *t*." The qualifications "unless I am prevented" or "unless I forget about the time" do not belong to the inference as a commitment. Should the commitment not be fulfilled, however, they may be offered as *excuses*. It is only when we look at the case from the point of view of a spectator ("third person") that the conclusion will have to be stated in the more guarded form of the agent's "setting himself" to do the action and will have to be subject to the qualifications about nonprevention and nonforgetfulness.

34. The compatibility problem is very clearly presented in Waismann 1953. The difficulties of the problem are set out in Malcolm 1968. The term Compatibility Thesis, as far as I know, was coined by Flew 1959.

35. "Drained of intentionality" means described in such a way that the behavior (movement) of A's body is not intentional under that description.

36. This is why the two-level solution advanced by Waismann, **and others**, does not solve the problem. Waismann distinguishes between action as "a series of movements" and as "something that has a purpose or meaning." Actions in the first sense, he says, are determined by (physiological) causes; actions in the second sense by motives and reasons. This view corresponds closely to the dis-

tinction made here between behavior as movement and as action. The two-level view of action (or, as I should prefer to say, behavior) is related, not uninterestingly, to Kant's view of the agent as a "citizen of two worlds," *viz.* the world of phenomena and that of noumena. On the view taken here, *action is,* although not exactly in the Kantian sense, *a noumenal idea.*

37. Von Wright 1963a, Ch. III, Sect. 3.

38. The divisions of actions into basic and nonbasic ones applies, be it observed, to *individual* and not to *generic* actions. (On this distinction, see von Wright 1963a, Ch. III, Sect. 2.) Whether an (individual) action is basic or not depends upon *how it is performed*—directly or by doing something else—on the individual occasion for its performance. As far as I can see, there exists no directly performable action whose result could not *also* be brought about by doing something else. If, therefore, basic actions are defined as originally in Danto 1963, p. 435, there would probably, contrary to Danto's thesis, not exist any basic actions at all.

39. What I have called "the counterfactual element in action" is thus *not* that certain changes would not happen were it not for the agent's making them happen. The element of counterfactuality consists in that the agent *confidently thinks* that certain changes will not occur unless he acts. This confidence has an experiential basis. But this does not show that a causal tie exists between certain changes (the results of his action) and his acting. Acting does not cause events in the world. To think that it does would be "animism." If an event is the result of an action which is *not* basic, then its cause is some other event which is the result of one of our basic actions. The results of basic actions again may have causes which are not themselves the results of any of our actions. Only seldom does an outside observer verify their operation when we are acting. And *we* cannot, for logical reasons, verify this, even if we could (all the time) watch what is going on in our brain.

40. Cf. Wittgenstein 1967a, Sect. 608.

IV. Explanation in History and the Social Sciences

1. On the importance of W*hat?* questions to historical explanation see Dray 1959.

Notes

2. The idea of "colligation under a new concept" plays a great role in William Whewell's philosophy of induction. See especially Whewell 1858, Ch. V. Interesting uses of the same idea in the philosophy of history are found in the writings of W. H. Walsh. See in particular Walsh 1942, pp. 133–135 and Walsh 1951, pp. 59–64.

3. This "law," the working of which is a main theme of Hegel's doctrine of being in the first part of *Logik*, can be regarded as a general antireductionist idea. The favorite examples are usually adduced from chemistry. (Cf. Engels 1878, Pt. I, Ch. XII and Engels, *Dialektik*, p. 84.) They are, however, of a very different nature from examples, allegedly of the same law, from social life. Such examples are the transformation of money into capital, analyzed by Marx in 1867/1894, or the transformation of bourgeois into proletarian democracy, sketched in Lenin 1918, Ch. V, Sect. 4. The law of the transmutation of quantity into quality seems to me to be a good example of the tendency of Hegel and writers in his tradition to heap under a common label a number of conceptually highly disparate things. (Cf. Winch 1958, pp. 72–73.) This tendency is partly responsible for the many ambivalences inherent in hegelian and, to an even greater extent, marxist thinking. One should also see against this background the tension between an interpretation considered orthodox and various forms of "revisionism."

4. The debate about causation in history derives much of its confusion and obscurity from a failure to separate the question of the appropriateness of a certain (causal) *terminology* from the question of the applicability of certain (causal) *categories* or concepts to historical research. The reasons which have been advanced against the use of causal language in history are very mixed. Sometimes it is considered that accepting the covering law model for history makes the use of ("old-fashioned") causal terminology obsolete—and that this is why we should (need) not speak about causes in history. Sometimes it is thought that causal terminology should be avoided just because of its linkage with the covering law model, which is then rejected. Conceptual clarity is seldom promoted by linguistic reform and it seems to me pointless and

Chapter IV

vain to protest or warn against the causal terminology commonly employed in history and social science. It is more to the point to warn against the use of the methodological label "causal explanation" in the human sciences. (Cf. above, Ch. III, Sect. 1, n. 4.) The most important point at issue, however, is whether, or to what extent, causal explanations in history and social science conform to subsumption-theoretic explanation patterns.

When Croce or Collingwood or Oakeshott (1933, p. 131) protest against causation in history, their protest is directed against the application to history of a category which is at home in the natural sciences. Croce (1938, p. 16) speaks of the "semplice e fondamentale verità . . . che il concetto di causa . . . è e deve rimanere estraneo alla storia, perché nato sul terreno delle scienze naturali e avente il suo ufficio nell'ámbito loro." When, against them, Mandelbaum (1938, 1942) defends the legitimacy of causal analysis and causal explanation in history this is partly in the name of an extended use of causal language, but partly also in the name of a view of causal relations as "bonds of dependence" between events which evidently is meant to be applicable to both the natural and the human sciences. A related view, assimilating causation in history to causation between natural events, is found in Cohen 1942.

In German one can make a useful distinction between "Kausalität" and "Ursächlichkeit" and associate the first term with a narrower ("scientific") and the second with a broader use of the English term "causation." Cf. Gadamer 1964, p. 200: "Es ist ein anderer Sinn von 'Ursache,' nicht der der Kausalität, was den Zusammenhang der Geschichte determiniert."

5. Once again it is appropriate to warn against the ambiguities of terminology here. If "causal explanation" in history is understood in a broad sense, not committed to the covering law theory, then sufficient conditions are certainly also "directly" relevant to the search for historical explanations. Explanatory analysis in terms of conditionship relations is as important, and the distinction between the various kinds of condition just as useful, in the study of human affairs as it is in the natural sciences. The difference is that conditionship relations which express nomic ties of humean

Notes

causation usually enter the explanations in history and social science in an *oblique* manner, meaning that the correctness of the explanation is not dependent on the truth of the nomic connection involved. (Cf. Ch. III, Sect. 1.) For the use of condition concepts in causal analysis and explanation in history see Dahl 1956, Marc-Wogau 1962, and Tranøy 1962.

6. On the causes of the First World War see the interesting, though often controversial, book by G. M. Thomson (1964). Thomson lays great emphasis on the "causal" roles of the new situations created as fortuitous consequences of various political actions.

7. It is, of course, not maintained that the actors on history's stage normally formulate practical arguments in words or thoughts when they act. *Sometimes,* however, they do this.

8. Marx's conception of the historical process is essentially an effort to trace the great changes in society back to changes of a technological nature. The clearest statement is perhaps to be found in the Introduction to Marx 1859. See also Elster 1969a, b.

9. The difference between the Greek and the Christian attitude to "nature" may be a case in point. The idea of man's domination over nature thanks to his insight into, and power to manipulate, causal mechanisms is connected in origin with the secularization of a Judeo-Christian religious tradition. But this process of secularization was, in its turn, conditioned by the development of the crafts and of weaponry and thus by changes of a technological character in the later Middle Ages.

10. Cf. Wittfogel 1932. The author makes a distinction between two types of forces of production (*Produktionskräfte*), viz. those which depend on social and those which depend on natural (geophysical) conditions. Wittfogel argues that Marx himself and some of the principal writers in his tradition had an acute sense of the basic importance of the geophysical conditions (*das Natur-moment*) to economic and social history. This awareness, the author thinks, is missing from the writings of many later "historical materialists" who place exclusive emphasis on the socially conditioned forces of production.

11. Some methodologists, it seems to me, misrepresent and

overestimate the importance of falsification to scientific theory-building. The primary role of falsification is in connection with various procedures characteristic mainly of the natural sciences and traditionally studied in inductive logic: the search for causes, the elimination of concurrent explanatory hypotheses, the design of "crucial experiments" to decide between rival theories, *etc.* In these procedures a relatively stable conceptual framework is presupposed for the purposes of describing and explaining phenomena. Changes in conceptual schemas, *e.g.* the adoption and discarding of paradigms in Kuhn's sense, is only obliquely, if at all, the result of "falsification."

12. Kuhn (1962) doubts whether the social sciences have yet reached a stage which is characterized by universally received paradigms—the overthrow of which and adoption of new paradigms constitute a "scientific revolution" (p. 15). The truth is probably that there are no *universal* paradigms in social science and that this is a feature which distinguishes it from natural science. But it is certainly also the case that marxist social science is paradigm dominated—although the development of marxist science testifies to many attempts to break away from paradigms. What marxists call "bourgeois" social science is probably molded more by paradigms than people reared in the traditional accumulative view of science as a uniformly growing body of facts and theories are inclined to admit. One can therefore with some justification speak of existing parallel types of social science. (Cf. Löwith 1932, p. 53.) They differ not so much in that they hold conflicting views about facts as in the paradigms which they adopt for purposes of description and explanation. This difference in paradigms reflects a difference in *ideology*. "Revolutions" in social science, therefore, are the results of ideology-critique.

13. The distinction which I am here making is *related* to the distinction which Hart (1961) makes between primary and secondary rules. It is a great merit of Hart's to have pointed out that a normative system such as a legal order is a union of the two types of rule. It does not possess the monistic character which, for example, Kelsen (1949) attributes to it, when he thinks that every legal norm can be reconstructed as a coercive norm, *i.e.* as

a norm providing for sanctions. Hart's attempt to characterize the secondary rules does not seem to me entirely successful, however.

14. With regard to the importance accorded to rules in sociological research it is interesting to compare Winch's idea of a social science with that of Durkheim. Both authors put strong emphasis on rules, but neither of them makes the distinction which I have made here between the two types of norm or rule. Durkheim apparently thinks of norms predominantly as rules of conduct which exert a normative pressure on behavior. Winch again is primarily concerned with rules which define institutions or constitute practices. One can relate this difference in emphasis to the difference generally between the "positivist" methodology of Durkheim and the "hermeneutic" methodology of Winch.

15. The point which I have tried to make here about the *essential incompleteness* of the historian's description of the past is more fully elaborated in Danto 1965b. See especially the brilliant chapter on narrative sentences, pp. 143–181.

16. See Löwith 1941, Pt. I, Ch. i; also Maurer 1965.

17. Cf. Buckley 1967, p. 18.

18. As noted before, in Ch. I, Sect. 10, cybernetics has made a strong impact on certain trends in modern marxist philosophy and social science. Cybernetics is very much "in fashion" in the socialist countries of Eastern Europe. In view of this I find it surprising that, to the best of my knowledge, very little has so far been done to reinterpret *systematically* the hegelian conceptual framework, inherited and developed by marxism, in the light of cybernetic or systems-theoretic ideas and terminology.

A systems-theoretic reinterpretation of hegelian logic does not necessarily lead to a "causalist" theory of scientific explanation. Cybernetic explanations in biology, *e.g.* an explanation of purposeful behavior on the lines of the classic paper by Rosenblueth, Wiener, and Bigelow (1943), are, I think, "causalist" or "mechanist" in the sense that they conform to a subsumption-theoretic or covering law model. But it does not follow that the use of cybernetic categories for the purpose of understanding social phenomena is, in this sense, "causalist." Phenomena involving intentionality and *genuine* teleology may also be accounted for in cybernetic terminology, as the example discussed in the text was meant to indicate.

19. Cf. Dahl 1956, p. 108.

20. Cf. Trotsky's well-known comment on a cold which he unexpectedly got at a critical moment of his political life (Carr 1961, p. 92). The problem of reconciling the working of "the iron law of history" with the capricious operations of chance always constituted a problem for marxist historical thinking. On this see Carr 1961, p. 95f.; Engels 1894.

21. Cf. Mill 1843, Bk. VI, Ch. iii, Sect. 2: "The actions of individuals could not be predicted with scientific accuracy." But for the purposes of political and social science, Mill adds, we can predict of the "collective conduct of masses" things which are "only probable when asserted of individual human beings indiscriminately selected."

22. Rapp 1968, p. 157f. For examples from the history of thought see also Keynes 1921, Ch. XXIX.

23. For a fuller discussion of the epistemological problems connected with the idea of the *Ausgleich des Zufalls* see von Wright 1941/1957, Ch. VII, Sect. 3.

24. Cf. Wittgenstein 1967b, p. 94: "Die Warhrscheinlichkeit hängt mit dem Wesen einer unvollständigen Beschreibung zusammen." Also Wittgenstein 1964, p. 293: "Das Gesetz der Wahrscheinlichkeit ist das Naturgesetz, was man sieht, wenn man blinzelt."

25. The term "historicism" is used in a confusing multitude of senses. (Cf. Carr 1961, p. 86.) Popper (1957) understands "by 'historicism' an approach to the social sciences which assumes that *historical prediction* is their principal aim" (p. 3). But not all authors whom he accuses of historicism are historicists in *this* sense, least of all Hegel, one of the main targets of Popper's onslaught.

26. Hegel's view of necessity in history is very decidedly a determinism of the intelligibility, not of the predictability, type. The necessity inherent in the historic process is conceptual, logical. (Cf. Litt 1953, p. 223.) This is also the view of philosophers of history in a hegelian vein such as Croce and Collingwood. As against this,

the marxist view of historical necessity is inherently ambiguous or ambivalent as between the two types. There is a rift in Marx's own thinking here. His thought seems to oscillate between a "scientistic" or "positivist" attitude to determinism, and a "hermeneutic" attitude. This ambivalence is reflected in the subsequent development of marxism. (Cf. above, Ch. I, n. 27.) Thus, for example, Kon (1964, Vol. I, pp. 290ff.) interprets the claim of historical materialism that history and the social process is governed by deterministic laws as a claim that historical events are predictable on the macrolevel. Others see in historical materialism a paradigm for making the past intelligible. (Cf. above, Sect. 4.) I think myself the latter is the more fruitful view.

27. *I.e.*, it must have been shown to be intelligible as action. Cf. Walsh 1959, p. 299.

28. See Foot 1957; also Westermarck 1906, Ch. XIII.

References

This bibliography does not aim at completeness, or even at listing all the more important publications in the field. It includes writings which I have consulted in the course of my work and found useful. Not all the publications listed here are actually mentioned or referred to in the notes.

I have used the following abbreviations: APQ—*American Philosophical Quarterly*; BJPS—*The British Journal for the Philosophy of Science*; JHI—*Journal of the History of Ideas*; JP—*The Journal of Philosophy*; MW—*Man and World*; PAS—*Proceedings of the Aristotelian Society*; PPR—*Philosophy and Phenomenological Research*; PQ—*The Philosophical Quarterly*; PR—*The Philosophical Review*; PS—*Philosophy of Science*; RM—*The Review of Metaphysics*.

Abel, Th. 1948. "The Operation called 'Verstehen'." *American Journal of Sociology 54*. Reprinted in and quoted from *Readings in the Philosophy of Science,* ed. by H. Feigl and M. Brodbeck. Appleton-Century-Crofts, New York, 1953.

Ackermann, R. 1965. "Deductive Scientific Explanation." *PS 32*.

—— 1967. "Explanations of Human Action." *Dialogue 6*.

References

—— 1969. "Mechanism, Methodology, and Biological Theory." *Synthese 20.*

—— and A. Stennes 1966. "A Corrected Model of Explanation." *PS 33.*

Ajdukiewicz, K. 1934. "Das Weltbild und die Begriffsapparatur." *Erkenntnis 4.*

Albert, H. 1968. *Traktat über kritische Vernunft.* J. C. B. Mohr, Tübingen.

Angel, R. B. 1967. "Explanation and Prediction: A Plea for Reason." *PS 34.*

Anscombe, G. E. M. 1957. *Intention.* Basil Blackwell, Oxford.

Apel, K. O. 1955. "Das Verstehen (eine Problemgeschichte als Begriffsgeschichte)." *Archiv für Begriffsgeschichte 1.*

—— 1966. "Wittgenstein und das Problem des hermeneutischen Verstehens." *Zeitschrift für Theologie und Kirche 63.*

—— 1967. *Analytic Philosophy of Language and the Geisteswissenschaften.* D. Reidel, Dordrecht-Holland. Originally published in German in *Philosophisches Jahrbuch 72,* 1965.

—— 1968. "Szientistik, Hermeneutik, Ideologie-Kritik." *MW 1.*

Aristotle. *The Nicomachean Ethics.*

Ashby, W. Ross. 1952. *Design for a Brain: The Origin of Adaptive Behaviour.* John Wiley & Sons, New York (2nd rev. ed. 1960).

—— 1956. *An Introduction to Cybernetics.* Chapman & Hall, London.

Ayala, F. J. 1970. "Teleological Explanation in Evolutionary Biology." *PS 37.*

Berlin, I. 1954. *Historical Inevitability.* Oxford University Press.

Black, M. 1955. "Why Cannot an Effect Precede Its Cause?" *Analysis 16.*

—— 1958. "Making Something Happen." In S. Hook (ed.) 1958.

Braithwaite, R. B. 1953. *Scientific Explanation.* Cambridge University Press.

Brandt, R., and J. Kim 1963. "Wants as Explanations of Actions." *JP 60.*

Broad, C. D. 1926. *The Philosophy of Francis Bacon.* Cambridge University Press.

References

—— 1930. "The Principles of Demonstrative Induction (I)."
Mind 39.

—— 1935. "Mechanical and Teleological Causation." *PAS*, Suppl.
Vol. *14*.

—— 1950. Critical Notice on Kneale 1949. *Mind* 59.

Brown, D. G. 1968. *Action*. Allen & Unwin, London.

Buckley, W. 1967. *Sociology and Modern Systems Theory*. Prentice-Hall, Englewood Cliffs, N.J.

—— (ed.) 1968. *Modern Systems Research for the Behavioral Scientist: A Sourcebook*. Aldine Publishing Company, Chicago.

Burks, A. W. 1951. "The Logic of Causal Propositions." *Mind* 60.

Burtt, E. A. 1924. *The Metaphysical Foundations of Modern Physical Science*. Kegan Paul, Trench, Trubner & Co., London (2nd rev. ed. 1932).

Campbell, N. 1921. *What Is Science?* References are to the reprint by Dover, New York, 1952.

Canfield, J. V. (ed.). 1966. *Purpose in Nature*. Prentice-Hall, Englewood Cliffs, N.J.

Carr, E. H. 1961. *What Is History?* Macmillan, London.

Cassirer, E. 1946. "Galileo's Platonism." In *Studies and Essays Offered in Homage to George Sarton*. Ed. by M. F. Ashley Montagu. Henry Schuman, New York.

Castañeda, H. N. 1960/1961. "Imperative Reasonings." *PPR* 21.

Caws, P. 1965. *The Philosophy of Science*. D. Van Nostrand, Princeton, N.J.

Chisholm, R. M. 1946. "The Contrary-to-Fact Conditional." *Mind* 55.

—— 1966. "Freedom and Action." In K. Lehrer (ed.) 1966.

—— and R. Taylor 1960. "Making Things to Have Happened." *Analysis* 20.

Churchland, P. M. 1970. "The Logical Character of Action-Explanations." *PR* 79.

Cohen, M. R. 1942. "Causation and its Application to History." *JHI* 3.

Collingwood, R. G. 1940. *An Essay on Metaphysics*. Oxford University Press.

References

—— 1946. *The Idea of History.* Oxford University Press.

Comte, A. 1830. *Cours de philosophie positive.*

—— 1844. *Discours sur l'esprit positif.*

—— 1851. *Le Système de politique positive.*

[Comte 1830 (the first two "Leçons") and 1844 are here quoted from the commented edition by Ch. le Verrier (Classiques Garnier, Paris, 1949).]

Cornelius, H. 1903. *Einleitung in die Philosophie.* B. G. Teubner, Leipzig.

—— 1931. "Zur Kritik der wissenschaftlichen Grundbegriffe." *Erkenntnis 2.*

Cowan, J. L. 1968. "Purpose and Teleology." *The Monist 52.*

Croce, B. 1938. *La Storia come Pensiero e come Azione.* Laterza & Figli, Bari.

Dahl, O. 1956. *Om årsaksproblemer i historisk forskning* (Problems of Causation in Historical Research). Universitetsforlaget, Oslo.

Danto, A. 1963. "What Can We Do?" *JP* 60.

—— 1965a. "Basic Actions." *APQ* 2.

—— 1965b. *Analytical Philosophy of History.* Cambridge University Press.

—— 1966. "Freedom and Forbearance." In K. Lehrer (ed.) 1966.

D'Arcy, E. 1963. *Human Acts.* Oxford University Press.

Daveney, T. F. 1966. "Intentions and Causes." *Analysis* 27.

David, A. 1965. *La cybérnetique et l'humain.* Gallimard, Paris.

Davidson, D. 1963. "Actions, Reasons and Causes." *JP* 60.

—— 1967. "Causal Relations." *JP* 64.

Derbolav, J. 1970. "Über die gegenwärtigen Tendenzen der Hegelaneignung." *Akten des XIV. Internationalen Kongresses für Philosophie Wien 2.-9. September 1968.* Band V. Herder, Wien.

Desan, W. 1965. *The Marxism of Jean-Paul Sartre.* Doubleday, Garden City, N.Y.

Dilthey, W. 1883. *Einleitung in die Geisteswissenschaften.*

—— 1894. *Ideen über eine beschreibende und zergliedernde Psychologie.*

—— 1900. "Die Entstehung der Hermeneutik."

—— 1905. *Die Jugendgeschichte Hegels.*

References

—— 1910. *Der Aufbau der geschichtlichen Welt in den Geistes-wissenschaften.*
[The above works are published in W. Dilthey, *Gesammelte Schriften* (I–VII), B. G. Teubner, Leipzig, 1914–1927.]

Dingler, H. 1931. "Über den Aufbau der experimentellen Physik." *Erkenntnis* 2.

—— 1953. "Was ist Konventionalismus?" *Actes du XIème Congrès International de Philosophie*, vol. 5. North-Holland, Amsterdam.

Donagan, A. 1962. *The Later Philosophy of R. G. Collingwood.* Oxford University Press.

—— 1964/1966. "The Popper-Hempel Theory Reconsidered." In W. H. Dray (ed.) 1966.

Dray, W. H. 1957. *Laws and Explanation in History.* Oxford University Press.

—— 1959. " 'Explaining What' in History." In P. Gardiner (ed.) 1959.

—— 1963. "The Historical Explanation of Actions Reconsidered." In S. Hook (ed.) 1963.

—— 1968. "On Explaining How-Possibly." *The Monist* 52.

—— (ed.) 1966. *Philosophical Analysis and History.* Harper and Row, New York.

Droysen, J. G. 1858. *Grundriss der Historik.*

—— 1857/1937. *Enzyklopädie und Methodologie der Geschichte.* [Both works are published in J. G. Droysen, *Historik*, ed. by R. Hübner, Oldenbourgh, Munich, 1937.]

Ducasse, C. J. 1925. "Explanation, Mechanism, and Teleology." *JP* 22.

—— 1926. "On the Nature and the Observability of the Causal Relation." *JP* 23.

—— 1957. "On the Analysis of Causality." *JP* 54.

—— 1961. "Concerning the Uniformity of Causality." *PPR* 22.

—— 1965. "Causation: Perceivable? or Only Inferred?" *PPR* 26.
[The above papers are reprinted in C. J. Ducasse, *Truth, Knowledge and Causation*, Routledge & Kegan Paul, London, 1968.]

Dummett, M. 1954. "Can an Effect Precede Its Cause?" *PAS*, Suppl. Vol. 28.

References

—— 1964. "Bringing About the Past." *PR* 73.

Durkheim, É. 1893. *De la division du travail social.*

—— 1894. *Les règles de la méthode sociologique.*

Eberle, R., D. Kaplan, and R. Montague 1961. "Hempel and Oppenheim on Explanation." *PS* 28.

Elster, J. 1969a. *Essays om Hegel og Marx.* Pax Forlag, Oslo.

—— 1969b. "Teknologi og historie." *Häften för kritiska studier* 2.

Eneroth, B. 1969/1970. "En tolkning av den marxistiska dialektiken" ("An Interpretation of Marxist Dialectics"), I–II. *Häften för kritiska studier* 2–3.

Engels, F. 1878. *Herrn Eugen Dührings Umwälzung der Wissenschaft* ("Anti-Dühring").

—— *Dialektik der Natur.* [Posth. publ.; ref. to English translation by J. B. S. Haldane, London, 1940.]

—— 1894. Letter to Starkenburg 25.I 1894. Ref. to *Karl Marx und Friedrich Engels, Ausgewählte Schriften* II. Dietz, Berlin, 1955.

Fain, H. 1963. "Some Problems of Causal Explanation." *Mind* 72.

Flew, A. 1954. "Can an Effect Precede Its Cause?" *PAS*, Suppl. Vol. 28.

—— 1959. "Determinism and Rational Behaviour." *Mind* 68.

Foot, Ph. 1957. "Free Will as Involving Determinism." *PR* 66.

Frischeisen-Köhler, M. 1912. "Wilhelm Dilthey als Philosoph." *Logos* 3.

Fromm, E. (ed.) 1965. *Socialist Humanism.* Doubleday, Garden City, N.Y.

Gadamer, H. G. 1960. *Wahrheit und Methode, Grundzüge einer philosophischen Hermeneutik.* J. C. B. Mohr, Tübingen.

—— 1964. "Kausalität in der Geschichte?" In *Ideen und Formen, Festschrift für Hugo Friedrich.* Vittorio Klostermann Verlag, Frankfurt/Main. Reprinted in *Kleine Schriften* I.

—— 1967. *Kleine Schriften* I–II. J. C. B. Mohr, Tübingen.

—— 1969. "Hermeneutik." In *Contemporary Philosophy* III, ed. by R. Klibansky. La Nuova Italia, Firenze.

References

—— (ed.) 1967. *Das Problem der Sprache*. Wilhelm Fink, Munich.

Gale, R. M. (ed.) 1968. *The Philosophy of Time*. Macmillan, London.

Galileo, G. 1628. *Dialoghi sui massimi sistemi tolemaico e copernicano*.

—— 1638. *Discorsi e dimostrazioni matematiche intorno à due nuove scienze*.

Gardiner, P. 1952. *The Nature of Historical Explanation*. Oxford University Press.

—— 1966. "Historical Understanding and the Empiricist Tradition." In *British Analytical Philosophy*, ed. by B. Williams and A. Montefiore. Routledge and Kegan Paul, London.

—— (ed.) 1959. *Theories of History*. The Free Press, Glencoe, Ill.

Gasking, D. 1955. "Causation and Recipes." *Mind 54*.

Gluck, S. E. 1955. "Do Statistical Laws Have Explanatory Efficacy?" *PS 22*.

Goodman, N. 1947. "The Problem of Counterfactual Conditionals." *JP 44*.

—— 1954. *Fact, Fiction and Forecast*. The Athlone Press, London.

Gramsci, A. 1953. "Il materialismo storico e la filosofia di Benedetto Croce." In *Opere II*. Feltrinelli, Milano.

Habermas, J. 1967. *Zur Logik der Sozialwissenschaften*. J. C. B. Mohr, Tübingen.

Hall, A. D. and R. E. Fagen. 1956. "Definitions of System." In Buckley (ed.) 1968.

Hamlyn, D. W. 1953. "Behaviour." *Philosophy 28*.

Hampshire, St. 1959. *Thought and Action*. Chatto and Windus, London.

Hanson, N. R. 1959. "On the Symmetry of Explanation and Prediction." *PR 68*.

Hart, H. L. A. 1961. *The Concept of Law*. Oxford University Press.

Hartmann, N. 1923. "Aristoteles und Hegel." Printed in N. Hartmann, *Kleinere Schriften II*. De Gruyter, Berlin, 1957.

—— 1951. *Teleologisches Denken*. De Gruyter, Berlin.

Hegel, G. W. F. 1807. *Phänomenologie des Geistes*.

213

References

—— 1812/1816. *Wissenschaft der Logik.*

—— 1830. *Enzyklopädie der philosophischen Wissenschaften* (3rd ed.).

—— *Jenenser Logik, Metaphysik und Naturphilosophie.* [Published posthumously; ed. by G. Lasson. Felix Meiner, Leipzig, 1923.]

Hempel, C. G. 1942. "The Function of General Laws in History." *JP 39.*

—— 1959. "The Logic of Functional Analysis." In *Symposium on Sociological Theory*, ed. by L. Gross. Harper and Row, New York.

—— 1962. "Deductive-Nomological *vs.* Statistical Explanation." In *Minnesota Studies in the Philosophy of Science* (III), ed. by H. Feigl and G. Maxwell. University of Minnesota Press.

—— 1962/1966. "Explanation in Science and in History." In W. H. Dray (ed.) 1966.

—— 1965. "Aspects of Scientific Explanation." In *Aspects of Scientific Explanation and other Essays in the Philosophy of Science.* The Free Press, New York. Includes also Hempel 1942, 1959, and Hempel-Oppenheim 1948.

—— and P. Oppenheim 1948. "Studies in the Logic of Explanation." *PS 15.*

Henderson, G. P. 1968. "Predictability in Human Affairs." In Vesey (ed.) 1968.

Hobart, R. E. 1930. "Hume without Scepticism (I–II)." *Mind 39.*

Hook, S. (ed.) 1958. *Determinism and Freedom.* New York University Press.

—— (ed.) 1963. *Philosophy and History.* New York University Press.

Hume, D. 1739. *A Treatise on Human Nature.*

—— 1748. *An Enquiry Concerning the Human Understanding.*

Iseminger, G. 1969. "Malcolm on Explanations and Causes." *Philosophical Studies 20.*

Jaeger, W. 1934. *Paideia* I. Walter de Gruyter, Berlin. Engl. transl. Basil Blackwell, Oxford, 1939.

Jarvis, J. 1962. "Practical Reasoning." *PQ 12.*

References

Johnson, W. E. 1921/1924. *Logic* I–III. Cambridge University Press.

Kaila, E. 1956. *Terminalkausalität als Grundlage eines unitarischen Naturbegriffs*. I. Acta Philosophica Fennica 10.

Kaufmann, W. 1965. *Hegel*. Doubleday, Garden City, N.Y.

Kelsen, H. 1941. *Vergeltung und Kausalität, eine soziologische Untersuchung*. W. P. Van Stockum & Zoon, The Hague.

—— 1949. *General Theory of Law and State*. Harvard University Press, Cambridge, Mass.

Kenny, A. 1963. *Action, Emotion and Will*. Routledge and Kegan Paul, London.

—— 1966. "Practical Inference." *Analysis 26*.

Keynes, J. M. 1921. *A Treatise on Probability*. Macmillan, London.

Kim, J. 1963. "On the Logical Conditions of Inductive Explanation." *PS 30*.

Kirschenmann, R. R. 1969. *Information and Reflection, On Some Problems of Cybernetics and How Contemporary Dialectical Materialism Copes with Them*. D. Reidel, Dordrecht-Holland.

Klaus, G. 1961. *Kybernetik in philosophischer Sicht*. Dietz Verlag, Berlin.

Kneale, W. 1949. *Probability and Induction*. Oxford University Press.

—— 1961. "Universality and Necessity." *BJPS 12*.

Kolnai, A. 1968. "Agency and Freedom." In Vesey (ed.) 1968.

Kon, I. S. 1964. *Die Geschichtsphilosophie des 20. Jahrhunderts* I–II. Akademie-Verlag, Berlin.

Koyré, A. 1939. *Études galiléennes* I–III. Hermann Éditeurs, Paris.

Krajewski, W. 1963. "Spory i szkoły w filozofii marksistowskiej" ("Schools and Disputes within Marxism"). In *Szkice filozoficzne* (*Philosophical Sketches*). Warsaw.

Kuhn, Th. S. 1962. *The Structure of Scientific Revolutions*. University of Chicago Press.

Kusý, M. 1970. "Szientismus oder Anthropologismus in der marxistischen Philosophie." *Akten des XIV. Internationalen Kongresses für Philosophie Wien 2.-9. September 1968*. Band V. Herder, Wien.

References

Lagerspetz, K. 1959. *Teleological Explanations and Terms in Biology*. Ann. Zool. Soc. 'Vanamo' XIX:6, Helsinki.

Lange, O. 1962. *Całość i rozwój w świetle cybernetyki*. Państwowo Wydawnictwo Naukowe, Warszawa. Engl. transl. *Wholes and Parts, A General Theory of System Behaviour*. Pergamon Press, Oxford.

Lauener, H. 1962. *Die Sprache in der Philosophie Hegels*. Paul Haupt, Bern.

Lehrer, K. (ed.) 1966. *Freedom and Determinism*. Random House, New York.

Lenin, V. I. 1909. *Materializm i Empiriokrititsizm* (*Materialism and Empiro-Criticism*).

—— 1918. *Gosudarstvo i revolyutsia* (*State and Revolution*).

Lerner, D. (ed.) 1965. *Cause and Effect*. The Free Press, New York.

Lewin, K. 1930/1931. "Der Übergang von der aristotelischen zur galileischen Denkweise in Biologie und Psychologie." *Erkenntnis 1*.

Litt, Th. 1953. *Hegel, Versuch einer kritischen Erneuerung*. Quelle & Meyer, Heidelberg.

Losano, M. G. 1969. *Giuscibernetica, macchine e modelli cibernetici nel diritto*. Einaudi, Torino.

Louch, A. R. 1963. "The Very Idea of a Social Science." *Inquiry 6*.

—— 1966. *Explanation and Human Action*. Basil Blackwell, Oxford.

Lukács, G. 1948. *Der junge Hegel*. Europa Verlag, Zürich.

—— 1955. "Zur philosophischen Entwicklung des jungen Marx," *Deutsche Zeitschrift für Philosophie 2*.

Löwith, K. 1932. "Max Weber und Karl Marx," I–II. *Archiv für Sozialwissenschaft und Sozialpolitik 67*.

—— 1941. *Von Hegel zu Nietsche*. Europa Verlag, Zürich.

MacIntyre, A. 1957. "Determinism." *Mind 66*.

—— 1966. "The Antecedents of Action." In *British Analytical Philosophy*, ed. by B. Williams and A. Montefiore. Routledge and Kegan Paul, London.

Mackie, J. L. 1965. "Causes and Conditions." *APQ 2*.

References

——— 1966. "The Direction of Causation." *PR* 75.

Malcolm, N. 1967. Rev. of Ch. Taylor 1964. *PR* 76.

——— 1968. "The Conceivability of Mechanism." *PR* 77.

Mandelbaum, M. 1938. *The Problem of Historical Knowledge*. Liveright Publishing Corporation, New York.

——— 1942. "Causal Analysis in History." *JHI* 3.

Marc-Wogau, K. 1962. "On Historical Explanation." *Theoria* 28.

Marcuse, H. 1932. *Hegels Ontologie und die Grundlegung einer Theorie der Geschichtlichkeit*. Vittorio Klostermann Verlag, Frankfurt am Main.

——— 1941. *Reason and Revolution: Hegel and the Rise of Social Theory*. Oxford University Press.

Marković, M. 1969. "Basic Characteristics of Marxist Humanism." *Praxis* 5.

Martin, J. M. 1969. "Another Look at the Doctrine of Verstehen." *BJPS* 20.

Marx, K. 1859. *Zur Kritik der politischen Ökonomie*.

——— 1867/1894. *Das Kapital* I–III.

Maurer, R. K. 1965. *Hegel und das Ende der Geschichte*. W. Kohlhammer Verlag, Stuttgart.

Maxwell, N. 1968. "Can There be Necessary Connections between Successive Events?" *BJPS* 19.

Mayr, E. 1965. "Cause and Effect in Biology." In D. Lerner (ed.) 1965.

McCormick, S. and I. Thalberg. 1967. "Trying." *Dialogue* 6.

Melden, A. I. 1961. *Free Action*. Routledge and Kegan Paul, London.

Mill, J. St. 1843. *A System of Logic*.

——— 1865. "August Comte and Positivism." *Westminster Review*.

Nagel, E. 1951. "Mechanistic Explanation and Organismic Biology." *PPR* 11.

——— 1953. "Teleological Explanation and Teleological Systems." *Readings in the Philosophy of Science*, ed. by H. Feigl and M. Brodbeck. Appleton-Century-Crofts, New York.

——— 1961. *The Structure of Science*. Harcourt, Brace and World, New York.

217

References

—— 1965. "Types of Causal Explanation in Science." In D. Lerner (ed.) 1965.

Nerlich, G. C. and W. A. Suchting. 1967. "Popper on Law and Natural Necessity." *BJPS 18*.

Neurath, O. 1931. *Empirische Soziologie.* Julius Springer, Wien.

Oakeshott, M. 1933. *Experience and Its Modes.* Cambridge University Press.

Pears, D. 1968. "Desires as Causes of Actions." In Vesey (ed.) 1968.

Poincaré, H. 1902. *La science et l'hypothèse.* Flammarion, Paris.

Popper, K. 1935. *Logik der Forschung.* Julius Springer, Vienna.

—— 1945. *The Open Society and Its Enemies* I–II. Routledge and Kegan Paul, London.

—— 1957. *The Poverty of Historicism.* Routledge and Kegan Paul, London.

—— 1967. "A Revised Definition of Natural Necessity." *BJPS 18*.

Pritchard, H. A. 1945. "Acting, Willing, Desiring." *Moral Obligation: Essays and Lectures.* Oxford University Press, 1949.

Quetelet, A. 1846. *Lettres sur la theórie des probabilités appliquée aux sciences morales et politiques.*

—— 1848. *Du système sociale et des lois qui le regnissent.*

Radnitzky, G. 1968. *Contemporary Schools of Metascience* I–II. Akademiförlaget, Gothenburg.

Rapp, Fr. 1968. *Gesetz und Determination in der Sowjetphilosophie.* D. Reidel, Dordrecht-Holland.

Reid, Th. 1788. *Essays on the Active Powers of Man.*

Rescher, N. 1963. "Discrete State Systems, Markov Chains, and Problems in the Theory of Scientific Explanation and Prediction." *PS 30*.

—— 1966. "Practical Reasoning and Values." *PQ 16*.

Rosenblueth, A. and N. Wiener. 1950. "Purposeful and Non-Purposeful Behaviour." *PS 17*. Reprinted in Buckley (ed.) 1968.

Rosenblueth, A., N. Wiener, and J. Bigelow. 1943. "Behaviour,

References

Purpose, and Teleology." *PS* 10. Reprinted in Canfield (ed.) 1966 and Buckley (ed.) 1968.

Russell, B. 1912/1913. "On the Notion of Cause." *PAS* 13. Quoted from *Mysticism and Logic*, Penguin Books, London, 1953.

Sartre, J. P. 1960. *Critique de la Raison Dialectique* I. Gallimard, Paris.

Schaff, A. 1961. *Marksizm a egzystencjalizm* (*Marxism and Existentialism*). Warsaw.

Scheffler, I. 1957. "Explanation, Prediction, and Abstraction." *BJPS* 7.

Schütz, A. 1932. *Der sinnhafte Aufbau der sozialen Welt, eine Einleitung in die verstehende Soziologie.* Julius Springer, Wien.

—— 1962. *Collected Papers: I. The Problem of Social Reality.* Ed. by M. Natanson. Martinus Nijhoff, The Hague.

—— 1964. *Collected Papers: II. Studies in Social Theory.* Ed. by A. Brodersen. Martinus Nijhoff, The Hague. Includes in translation a considerable portion of Schütz 1932.

Scriven, M. 1959. "Truisms as the Grounds for Historical Explanation." In P. Gardiner (ed.) 1959.

—— 1964. "The Structure of Science." Critical study of Nagel 1961. *RM* 17.

Simmel, G. 1892. *Die Probleme der Geschichtsphilosophie.* Duncker & Humblot, Leipzig.

—— 1918. *Vom Wesen des historischen Verstehens.* E. S. Mittler & Sohn. Berlin.

Simon, H. 1952. "On the Definition of the Causal Relation." *JP* 49.

—— 1953. "Causal Ordering and Identifiability." *Studies in Econometric Method,* ed. by W. C. Hood and T. C. Koopmans. John Wiley & Sons, New York. Reprinted in Lerner (ed.) 1965. References are to Lerner (ed.) 1965.

—— and N. Rescher 1966. "Cause and Counterfactual." *PS* 33.

Simon, J. 1966. *Das Problem der Sprache bei Hegel.* W. Kohlhammer Verlag, Berlin.

Skjervheim, H. 1959. *Objectivism and the Study of Man.* Universitetsvorlaget, Oslo.

References

Skolimowski, H. 1965. "Analytical Linguistic Marxism in Poland." *JHI 26*. Reprinted in H. Skolimowski, *Polish Analytical Philosophy*. Routledge & Kegan Paul, London, 1967.

Stegmüller, W. 1969. *Probleme und Resultate der Wissenschaftstheorie. I. Wissenschaftliche Erklärung und Begründung*. Springer Verlag, Berlin.

Stein, A. 1913. *Der Begriff des Geistes bei Dilthey*. Max Drechsel, Bern.

Stoutland, F. 1968. "Basic Actions and Causality." *JP 65*.

––––– 1970. "The Logical Connection Argument." *APQ 7*.

Suchting, W. A. 1967. "Deductive Explanation and Prediction Revisited." *PS 34*.

Suppes, P. 1970. *A Probabilistic Theory of Causality*. North-Holland, Amsterdam.

Taylor, Ch. 1964. *The Explanation of Behaviour*. Routledge and Kegan Paul, London.

––––– 1966. "Marxism and Empiricism." In *British Analytical Philosophy*, ed. by B. Williams and A. Montefiore. Routledge and Kegan Paul, London.

Taylor, R. 1950a. "Comments on a Mechanistic Conception of Purposefulness." *PS 17*.

––––– 1950b. "Purposeful and Non-Purposeful Behavior: A Rejoinder." *PS 17*.

––––– 1966. *Action and Purpose*. Prentice-Hall, Englewood Cliffs, N.J.

Thomson, G. M. 1964. *The Twelve Days*. Hutchinson, London.

Tranøy, K. E. 1962. "Historical Explanation: Causes and Conditions." *Theoria 28*.

Vanquickenborne, M. 1969. "An Analysis of Causality in Everyday Language." *Logique et Analyse 12*.

Vesey, G. N. A. (ed.) 1968. *The Human Agent*. Macmillan, London.

Wach, J. 1926/1933. *Das Verstehen, Grundzüge einer Geschichte der hermeneutischen Theorie im 19. Jahrhundert I–III*. J. C. B. Mohr, Tübingen.

References

Waismann, Fr. 1953. "Language Strata." *Logic and Language*. 2nd Series, ed. by A. Flew. Basil Blackwell, Oxford.

Wallace, J. D. 1969. "Practical Inquiry." *PR 78*.

Walsh, W. H. 1942. "The Intelligibility of History." *Philosophy 27*.

—— 1951. *An Introduction to the Philosophy of History*. Hutchinson, London.

—— 1959. " 'Meaning' in History". In P. Gardiner (ed.) 1959.

—— 1962/1963. "Historical Causation." *PAS 63*.

Weber, M. 1913. "Über einige Kategorien der verstehenden Soziologie." *Logos 4*.

—— 1921. *Wirtschaft und Gesellschaft, Grundriss der verstehenden Soziologie*. 4th ed., J. C. B. Mohr, Tübingen, 1956.

——. *Gesammelte Aufsätze zur Wissenschaftslehre*. J. C. B. Mohr, Tübingen, 1922. (Contains Weber 1913.)

Westermarck, E. 1906. *The Origin and Development of the Moral Ideas* I. Macmillan, London.

Whewell, W. 1858. *Novum Organon Renovatum* (3rd ed.). John W. Parker & Son, London.

White, A. R. 1967. *The Philosophy of Mind*. A. A. Knopf, New York.

Whiteley, C. H. 1968. "Mental Causes." In Vesey (ed.) 1968.

Wiener, N. 1948. *Cybernetics*. The M.I.T. Press, Cambridge, Mass.

Wilenius, R. 1967. *Filosofia ja politiikka* (*Philosophy and Politics*). Tammi, Helsinki.

Winch, P. 1958. *The Idea of a Social Science and Its Relation to Philosophy*. Routledge and Kegan Paul, London.

—— 1964a. "Understanding a Primitive Society." *APQ 1*.

—— 1964b. "Mr. Louch's Idea of a Social Science." *Inquiry 7*.

Windelband, W. 1894. "Geschichte und Naturwissenschaft." Reprinted in *Präludien*, 3rd ed., J. C. B. Mohr, Tübingen, 1907.

Wittfogel, K. A. 1932. "Die natürlichen Ursachen der Wirtschaftsgeschichte" I–III. *Archiv für Sozialwissenschaft und Sozialpolitik 67*.

Wittgenstein, L. 1921/1922. *Tractatus logico-philosophicus*. Kegan Paul, London.

—— 1953. *Philosophische Untersuchungen*. Basil Blackwell, Oxford.

—— 1964. *Philosophische Bemerkungen*. Basil Blackwell, Oxford.

References

—— 1967a. *Zettel*. Basil Blackwell, Oxford.

—— 1967b. *Gespräche, aufgezeichnet von Friedrich Waismann,* ed. by B. F. McGuinness. Suhrkamp, Frankfurt am Main.

—— 1969. *Philosophische Grammatik*. Suhrkamp, Frankfurt am Main.

Von Wright, G. H. 1941/1957. *The Logical Problem of Induction,* 2nd rev. ed. Basil Blackwell, Oxford.

—— 1951. *A Treatise on Induction and Probability*. Routledge and Kegan Paul, London.

—— 1957. "On Conditionals." *Logical Studies*. Routledge and Kegan Paul, London.

—— 1963a. *Norm and Action*. Routledge and Kegan Paul, London.

—— 1963b. "Practical Inference." *PR* 72.

—— 1965. " 'And Next.' " *Acta Philosophica Fennica 18.*

—— 1968a. " 'Always.' " *Theoria 34.*

—— 1968b. "The Logic of Practical Discourse." In *Contemporary Philosophy* I, ed. by R. Klibansky. La Nuova Italia, Firenze.

—— 1968c. *An Essay in Deontic Logic and the General Theory of Action*. North-Holland, Amsterdam.

—— 1969. *Time, Change and Contradiction*. Cambridge University Press.

Yolton, J. W. 1966. "Agent Causality." *APQ* 3.

Name Index

223

Name Index

Name Index

Marx, K., 7, 31, 160, 173, 174,
  183, 200, 202, 206
Maurer, R. K., 204
Maxwell, N., 178
Mayr, E., 193
Melden, A. I., 181, 195
Mill, J. St., 3, 4, 10, 171, 172,
  173, 175, 176, 184, 185,
  205
Mommsen, Th., 3
Montague, R., 178

Nagel, E., 17, 36, 56, 177, 183,
  187, 188, 190, 192
Nerlich, G. C., 178
Neurath, O., 182
Newton, I., 3

Oakeshott, M., 26, 28, 201
Oppenheim, P., 182

Pears, D., 181
Plato, 2
Poincaré, H., 178
Popper, K., 24, 164, 169, 174,
  175, 176, 178, 179, 184,
  205
Pritchard, H. A., 194

Radnitzky, G., 182
von Ranke, L., 3
Rapp, Fr., 174, 205
Rask, R., 3
Reid, Th., 189
Rescher, N., 185, 196
Rickert, H., 5
Rosenblueth, A., 16, 17, 177, 204
Russell, B., 9, 35, 36, 37, 38,
  183, 190

Sartre, J. P., 31, 183
Schaff, A., 182
Scheffler, I., 169
Schütz, A., 181
Scriven, M., 176, 184, 187

Simmel, G., 5, 6, 173
Simon, H., 191
Simon, J., 182
Skolimowski, H., 182
Stegmüller, W., 181
Stein, A., 172
Stennes, A., 178
Stoutland, F., 189, 195
Suchting, W. A., 178
Suppes, P., 36, 176, 183

Taylor, Ch., vii, 27, 28, 174,
  195, 196
Taylor, R., 177, 185
Thalberg, I., 197
Thomson, G. M., 202
Tranøy, K. E., 202
Trotsky, L., 205
Tylor, E., 3

Vanquickenborne, M., 184
Vesalius, A., 3
Vesey, G. N. A., 181

Wach, J., 172, 182
Waismann, Fr., 198
Wallace, J. D., 180
Walsh, W. H., 200, 206
Weber, M., 5, 7, 28, 173
Westermarck, E., 206
Whewell, W., 200
White, A. R., 195
Whiteley, C. H., 181
Wiener, N., 16, 17, 177, 204
Wilenius, R., 174, 181
Winch, P., 28, 29, 181, 200, 204
Windelband, W., 5, 172
Wittfogel, K. A., 202
Wittgenstein, L., 9, 28, 29, 30,
  33, 44, 45, 182, 195, 198,
  199, 205
Wood, A., 197

Yolton, J. W., 181

225

Subject Index

226

Subject Index

Subject Index

Subject Index

Subject Index